MAKING
THE GRADE

by **STAN OSBORNE**

Published by
Legends Publishing
18 Darby Crescent
Sunbury-on-Thames
Middlesex
TW16 5LA

E-mail david@legendspublishing.net
Web www.legendspublishing.net

CONTENTS

Dedicated to all those kids who could have made the grade... but didn't.

Acknowledgements
To my wife Jill and my mate Andrew Hill for their unstinting encouragement and support throughout, not least their proof reading. To David Starsky and his colleagues from the Everton FC Heritage Society for their help with my research. To Mal Jenkin for his help with my search for photos from the era. To Ronny Goodlass for his help and for agreeing to write the Foreword. To David Lane of Legends Publishing for his help in getting my book into print, and Rita Lane for her proof-reading help.

References
Everton, Player by Player, Ivan Ponting (Guinness Publishing 1992)
Everton, The Official Complete Record, Steve Johnson (deCourbetin Books 2010) www.evertonresults.com, www.evertonfc.com, www.theeverton-collection.com

FOREWORD

I have always considered myself extremely fortunate to have realised my ambition to pull on the famous royal blue jersey of Everton's first-team back in the 1970's and later on to be part of the Goodison Park coaching staff under Joe Royle's tenure as manager. I have also had the pleasure of being a match day commentator on Everton matches for Radio Merseyside over the past 15 years and have observed with interest the emerging talent as players have made their way from the Goodison production line into the first-team during that time.

I was lucky enough to graduate from The School of Science under Harry Catterick during a very special time for the club. Many promising and talented youngsters passed through the club during that era and Stan Osborne was one of the lads in my particular intake in 1969. Making The Grade tells of the adventures, trials and tribulations of life as an apprentice at that time. The hard toil on the training pitch, the tedious graft in the boot room were the downside, but the excitement of working your way through the junior ranks was the real thrill and they are all there described in minute detail. So is the euphoria of rubbing shoulders with The Holy Trinity of Kendall, Ball and Harvey and being in the company of the likes of Brian Labone, Joe Royle, Gordon West and even Harry Catterick himself. All true legends at the club who we had supported from the terraces only a matter of months before we signed as apprentices

The players, coaching staff, grounds staff and Management all come to life as Stan recounts the progress of the first-team as Everton clinched the First Division Title in 1969/70. At the same time the untold story of the progress the apprentices were making behind the scenes in the 'A' and 'B' teams is described, as well as some of the more amusing and outlandish activities and incidents we were involved in. It is an informative window into the past that looks at how young footballers had to face the highs and lows of life at the grass roots of the club then. A light is shone onto the triumph and joy for some as they made it to a full professional contract and onto the inevitable heartbreak for most of the others along with how each outcome was faced by the people concerned, with Stan's story taking centre stage.

On a personal level, Making The Grade brings back some fond memories of being a youngster at Everton. I am sure Evertonians of all ages and football fans everywhere will enjoy looking back at a brief period in the history of a great football club during an era that was so very different to today's Premier League.

Ronny Goodlass

INTRODUCTION

From humble beginnings to, well... humble endings. This is a story of football's wannabes, nearly men and might have beens – and there are a lot more of them than the David Beckhams, Wayne Rooneys and Steven Gerrards of this world. For thousands of football-mad kids over the years, who stood on the starting line in the race to become professional footballers alongside future internationals and household names, their story wasn't quite the same.

Somehow, for many different reasons, their promising careers remained just that – promising. While their famous peers found fame and fortune after making the grade, the also-rans only found the exit door and the scrapheap of the game's newest shiny prototypes.

The bookshop shelves are full of biographies and auto-biographies of the great players of the present and the past who graced our national sport at its pinnacle. But what of the young hopefuls who only got a toe onto the first rung of the football ladder and managed merely a worms-eye view of the beautiful game? Theirs is the forgotten story that is never heard, but is equally relevant because, just as the stars of the game emerged from the same working class roots to portray the glamour and fulfilment of their dreams, the kids who didn't make the grade provide a very different picture. However, their story contains just as much bravery, honest toil, commitment, joy and heartache.

This book harks back to a different era; an era before multi million pound transfer deals and contracts. Before the advent of the Premier League, Sky Sports and billionaire club owners. It looks back to a more innocent time when it felt as if football clubs and their stars still belonged to the fans instead of being at the mercy of players' agents and foreign takeovers.

This is an account of my brief experience as one of the young hopefuls at Everton Football Club during that era, but it could just as well be about any kid who started off with the footballing world at their feet, but just like the vast majority of other fledgling professional players, ended up with the weight of the world on their shoulders. This is a football story first and foremost, but as any ex-pro or apprentice pro of a certain age will tell you, actually making the grade in those days was about a lot more than just playing football. Making the grade then was just as much to do with coping with the minutiae of the 'upstairs, downstairs' life as a young footballer and the unexpected challenges, disappointments and knock about humour you were subjected to and the help, compassion and support, often from the most unlikely of sources, which enabled you to survive.

****

The 1968 FA Cup Final between Everton and West Bromwich Albion was a defining moment in my life. When Jeff Astle scored what proved to be the winning goal and the final whistle blew, it all became crystal clear. At the age of 14, out of the anguish, bitter disappointment and crushed dreams of that day, I knew what I suspected I'd always known – that one day I would sign for Everton Football Club as an apprentice professional footballer.

SEASON 1968/69
TALENT SPOTTING

In many ways, the 1968/1969 Season was a significant one for Harry Catterick's Everton but, more importantly for me and my footballing dreams, it was a crucial one. While Catterick continued with the latest phase of rebuilding his 1963 Championship Winning squad, I was busy proving myself as a promising schoolboy footballer on Merseyside with the latest Kirkby Schools FA Under 15 side, which was gaining recognition nationally amongst the scouts from Football League Clubs as a hotbed for new talent.

Since winning the League Title five years previously, Everton had maintained their position amongst the elite English clubs challenging for honours, finishing in the top six positions in the top division each year with the exception of 1966, when they lifted the FA Cup in the famous final at Wembley after coming back from 2-0 down to win 3-2 against Sheffield Wednesday. Throughout that time Everton's policy had been to gradually discard and replace older members of the squad such as Roy Vernon, Jimmy Gabriel, Alex Scott and Brian Harris. By the time the 68/69 season began, these and other renowned Everton stars like Alex (The Golden Vision) Young, Ernie Hunt and '66 FA Cup Final scorers Derek Temple and Mike Trebilcock were no longer at the club.

In fact the only remaining first-team players from 1963 championship winning squad were club captain Brian Labone, goalkeeper Gordon West and left winger Johnny Morrissey. Catterick's squad had been transformed through the purchase in the transfer market of Alan Ball after the 1966 World Cup from Blackpool for a then British record fee. He stole Howard Kendall from under the nose of Bill Shankly when he wanted to sign him for Liverpool from Preston North End. Sandy Brown was signed from Partick Thistle and little known Tommy Jackson from Glentoran was added to the squad.

Stan and Ray Pritchard selected to represent Lancashire schools

Everton at the time were considered to be the 'Merseyside Millionaires', with the spending power of the Moores family and the Littlewoods Pools Empire behind them. Many rivals at the time viewed the financial resources at Everton's disposal as an unfair advantage over most of the other clubs in England who didn't have a wealthy owner to bankroll the purchase of the top players in the league.

However, an emphasis on youth development was equally important at Goodison Park. Known as the 'School of Science' for their ability to produce players of the highest order, Everton's production line saw home grown talent such as John Hurst, Joe Royle, Colin Harvey, Andy Rankin, Tommy Wright, Jimmy Husband and Alan Whittle feeding through into the first-team squad to complement their big money signings.

So it was on this Everton production line that I had my sights firmly set as the 68/69 season for Kirkby schoolboys approached. Having been born in the Everton area and coming from a family of fanatical Evertonians, it was only natural that playing for Everton was my burning ambition. Moving out to football-mad Kirkby, the new Liverpool overspill town during the late 1950's also provided an environment where young footballers flourished.

The town planners who engineered these new towns during the post war slum clearance programme in many cities the length and breadth of the country got lots of things wrong. However, the one thing that we did have was space and as many football pitches as we could make use of. These pitches were put to good use with the vast numbers of youngsters on the estates honing their football skills from a very early age and most harbouring dreams of one day playing for either Everton or Liverpool; or at least being spotted by one of the scouts from League Clubs who were beating an increasingly well-worn path to this little corner of Merseyside to see school and representative matches.

So the agenda for the coming season was clear. For Harry Catterick and Everton it was the pursuit of more silverware; for me it was to do everything I could to get spotted by one of the Everton Scouts.

* * * *

Ultimately, Everton were to fall short of any silverware in all three domestic competitions. However, the season was not without its high points. Although the Toffees made a quick exit from the League Cup in round 4 after a replay against Derby County, their league form was promising up to the turn of the year, seeing them win 14 games including a 7-1 demolition of Leicester City, draw seven and lose only four matches.

So January 1969 left Everton well placed towards the top of Division 1 alongside Leeds, Liverpool and Arsenal with a favourable home tie against mid-table Ipswich to look forward to in the 3rd Round of the FA Cup. It was the FA Cup run that year that proved to be a sign of things to come. After disposing of Ipswich, further home ties against Coventry and Bristol Rovers resulted in Everton being drawn away against Manchester United in the quarter final. Over 63,000 packed into Old Trafford to see Everton squeeze into the Villa Park semi-final with Joe Royle scoring the only goal of the game. But mine and all other Evertonians' dreams of returning to Wembley for a second successive year were dashed when eventual winners, Manchester City, won a scrappy game 1-0 to qualify for the final against Leicester City. Another great FA Cup campaign providing food for thought and hope for the future.

Another positive feature of the season was the form and goal scoring efforts of key players. Joe Royle led the way with 18 goals, Alan Ball scored 15 with Jimmy Husband weighing in with nine before the new year. Royle and Husband continued in the same vein with them netting 29 and 20 times respectively by the end of the season. But even this tally wasn't enough to secure another league championship for Harry Catterick and Everton had to settle for third place behind Champions, Leeds United inspired by Don Revie and Bill Shankly's Liverpool.

Another fact had not escaped my notice having watched virtually all of Everton's home matches that season and quite a few reserve games. Another batch of young players had been introduced and blooded in the first-team squad from within the youth set-up, notably Alan Whittle, Roger Kenyon, Gerry Humphreys, Frank Darcy and Terry Darracott. Further encouragement, if I needed any, that if I tried hard enough and was really lucky, I might follow in their footsteps one day.

* * * *

Trying hard was exactly what I did as a centre forward for Brookfield School U15's, coached expertly by PE Teacher Bob Downing. Under his guidance, a fair few of his team, including Phil Thompson (later of Liverpool and England), had progressed through to the Kirkby Schools U14 side during the previous season. After a very successful year as U14's, we were fancied to do well in our English Schools Trophy season due in part to the fact that the Kirkby Schools U15's had reached the last eight of the competition for the previous two years.

An increasing number of club scouts were also making regular visits to run the rule over the Kirkby-based talent that was emerging from the schoolboy ranks there. For example, Jimmy Redfearn had been signed as an apprentice pro by Bolton Wanderers in 1967 and the following season saw Peter Scott and Keith Williams sign for Everton while Dennis Mortimer and Alan Dugdale took up apprenticeships with Coventry City. At around the same time Terry MacDermott (later of Newcastle United and Liverpool) signed full-time for Bury FC.

Put in context, reaching the last eight in the country was a remarkable achievement for Kirkby Schools F.A., when you bear in mind that there were only three school teams (Brookfield, St Kevin's and Ruffwood) to provide schoolboy players for representative teams. Added to this was the remarkable fact that the Association had only been in existence a matter of eight years. This was in contrast to the long-established major forces of Liverpool Boys, Manchester Boys, Birmingham Boys and many other cities which had literally hundreds, if not thousands of boys to select from. But the streets and fields of Kirkby were a tough testing ground and if you made it through to the Kirkby Boys team in those days, you most certainly had the talent to compete with the larger associations.

So, when the Kirby Boys squad assembled at the start of the 1968/1969 season, Manager Vince Kelly and coaches John Channel and Terry Duffy made it clear that our objective was to emulate the previous two years and go on to win one of the competitions we were entered for that season. As well as the ESFA Trophy, we were also entered for the three other competitions; the Lancashire Schools Trophy, The Dimmer (Merseyside) Cup and, unusually, the Welsh Schools Shield by virtue of the Welsh Schools FA allowing counties bordering Wales to enter teams due to Welsh sides being allowed to enter the English equivalent.

Our season couldn't have got off to a better start as we thrashed Southport Boys 11-0 in the 2nd Round of the Dimmer Cup at the Kraft Food Sports Ground on Moorgate Lane, Kirkby. We continued strongly in the Welsh Schools Shield recording wins against Mid Cheshire, Stockport and Crewe.

Already scouts from a number of professional clubs including Liverpool, Manchester United, Everton, Burnley and Hull City were attending our matches. This prompted Vince Kelly and the other staff to call a meeting of the boys and their parents to offer advice about dealing with enquiries or approaches from clubs. Firstly, the boys were instructed not to have any dealings with scouts themselves as this was deemed to be highly irregular. We were told to refer any approaches directly to our parents or, in their absence, to the staff.

Parents were advised not to consider signing 'Schoolboy' or 'Pink' forms as these tied the boys to one particular club until they left school and prevented other clubs signing them even if they wanted to offer an apprentice profes-sional contract. A firm offer of an apprenticeship was by far the best option, we were all told. This information was to prove useful to a number of us as the season unfolded.

We progressed in the Lancashire Schools trophy beating Burnley Boys, went on to qualify for the final of the Welsh Schools Shield and reached the quar-ter final of the English Schools Trophy overcoming Crosby, Stretford and West Stanley after causing the shock of the year by knocking out the previous year's holders Manchester Boys at their own ground.

(Left to Right) Phil Thompson, Paul McEwan and Stan Osborne

13

On an individual level quite a few of the Kirkby lads, including myself, were now clearly of interest to the talent scouts who were following our games. Apart from our successful results for Kirkby Boys, several of us had been chosen for Lancashire County trials with myself, Eddie Avis, Ray Pritchard and Steve Gregson being selected to play for the county. Ray also had the distinction of being the first ever Kirkby schoolboy to gain England Schoolboy honours.

Liverpool were in contact with Phil Thompson's parents, Manchester United had expressed an interest in Captain, Dougie Roberts while Hull City had been in contact with Steve Gregson's parents and Burnley were also in contact with Eddie Avis and Mick Quinn's parents. Meanwhile Everton scout Jimmy Tansey, who had attended quite a few of our matches, had spoken to my dad and had invited me to attend training at their Bellefield Training complex on Tuesday and Thursday evenings along with Ray Pritchard, Paul McEwan and Eddie Avis.

As the season progressed, the interest and speculation amongst lads and parents alike intensified as our results and with them our reputations as promising talent continued to gather pace.

However, as the season reached its climax, so too did the quality of the opposition as we neared the sharp end of a very competitive season. Our Welsh Schools Shield final ended up in a 2-2 aggregate draw with Cardiff, meaning we shared this prestigious trophy. A disappointing 1-0 defeat away at Barnsley meant we were only able to equal the achievements of our pre-decessors by reaching the last eight of the English Schools Trophy. We were knocked out of the Lancashire Schools trophy by Liverpool who went on to be English Champions that year. However, we were able to gain revenge when we defeated Liverpool over two legs to win the Dimmer Cup in our last two games of the season.

So a fine season for Kirkby Boys saw us with two trophies providing a further demonstration of the talent being nurtured on the football pitches in the town. Needless to say, the progress being made by both Kirkby and Liverpool schoolboys was being followed closely by the local press as well as talent scouts. The following article, *'Powerful Impact Of Soccer Twins'* appeared in the *Liverpool Echo* at the end of the season highlighting what had been achieved.

'This week, by mutual arrangement, the Kirkby and Liverpool Schools' Football Associations, ended their 1968-69 fixtures. The great Liverpool exodus to Kirkby, before the inception of the Kirkby Schools' F.A., has reduced the L.S.F.A. reservoir of "boy power" but produced an entity very much akin to another "Liverpool Boys" team, if one judges by status, deportment and prowess.

Certainly this season Kirkby Boys have jousted with champions. Dismissing somewhat casually on their own ground, England and Lancashire Cup-holders

Stan – Kirkby Boys' centre-forward

Manchester Boys, before they could even reach the English Trophy Competition Proper, the Kirkby lads have since shared Welsh honours with Cardiff Boys, champions 12 times in 20 final appearances.

It took English semi-finalists Barnsley, at home, to check their English Trophy progress beyond the quarter finals, which they reached for the third season in succession, and the English Champions Liverpool, to prevent them collecting possibly, the Lancashire Cup. The Dimmer Cup, they took from the 1968-69 English Champions at their Grove Mount stronghold. Never before has this North West corner of Merseyside made such an impact on schoolboy football......'

All of the reports and accolades we received were avidly absorbed by us boys and our parents. Typically, Vince Kelly as manager, with the other members of the Kirkby Schools F.A. committee, including Terry Duffy, John Channel and Bob Downing were happy to stay out of any limelight without seeking any acknowledgement for their part in our success. But their contribution was enormous; organising everything for us from training, coaching and transport to fundraising and even, in some cases, making sure we had a decent pair of boots to play in! The commitment of the teachers and committee members and many more like them across the country over many years was what enabled the whole culture of schoolboy football to thrive. This in turn was what provided the platform for many young footballers to develop and formed the bedrock of recruitment into the professional game for virtually all clubs in England.

On a personal note, I was happy to take the recognition that a tally of 26 goals in 19 competitive games brought my way – especially if it meant that Everton were showing a definite interest in me as a prospective centre forward recruit to their junior ranks. Toward that end, it was with great relish that I attended the midweek training sessions, which Everton put on for promising schoolboy players at their Bellefield training ground.

Together with Kirkby Boys team-mates Ray Pritchard, Paul McEwan and Eddie Avis, I caught the two buses from Southdene, in Kirkby to the West Derby area of Liverpool where Everton had established their state-of-the-art training facilities. Tucked away, almost secretively, behind a rectangle of neat suburban semi-detached houses in this leafy corner of Liverpool, it was easy to miss the entrance gates, which were squeezed into a gap just the width of a team bus, between two of the houses bordering the complex.

During our first visit we were met by Arthur Proudler a cheerful, balding, smiling, tracksuited coach of about 40 who addressed us in a soft Birmingham lilt explaining what we could expect when training at Bellefield. We were impressed when we were shown around the facilities. Immediately inside the gates, the drive led past the Groundsman's house toward the modern grey brick built buildings. To the right of the driveway was a full-sized training pitch immaculately laid out with gleaming white posts on lush green turf.

16

Table tennis in the Players' Lounge at Bellefield

Beyond this pitch another equally impressive one was set out at right angles with just the one goal visible as it continued around the back of the main building. To the left of the driveway was an area which looked as if it was used for five-a-side matches and another narrower area of grass continued around the back of a massive structure which contained a large indoor all-weather gravel pitch. To the right of the building which housed the indoor pitch, a corridor connected it to a two story building containing the changing rooms on the ground floor. There were four in all, arranged in two pairs with luxurious communal shower and bathing facilities for each. A kit/boot room, drying facilities, a trainers/referee's changing room and a Physio and Treatment room completed the downstairs of the complex.

Upstairs we were shown the Players' Lounge, which contained a table-tennis table and an array of comfortable seats and chairs. Across the landing was another set of rooms, which housed the kitchen and dining facilities along with office accommodation including an area we weren't allowed into. The plate on the door saying 'Manager' needed no explanation.

As a wide-eyed, innocent 15 year old who had been a fanatical Evertonian all my life, I found the guided tour of the training ground a little bit awe-inspiring. If I was in any doubt about the size and stature of Everton, seeing and using the training ground and experiencing the environment first hand underlined the fortunate position our efforts for Kirkby Boys had placed us in and the opportunity that was presenting itself.

The training sessions themselves were nothing out of the ordinary or unusual and always took place in the indoor area. The trainer, usually Arthur Proudler, put the group, normally of about 16 schoolboys through a series of warm up exercises, followed by drills and practices designed to assess and improve our technical skills and ball control. This was always followed by a seven or eight-a-side indoor game, often under conditions, such as one or two-touch to sharpen up our play. We also noticed that the trainer or someone assisting would always be observing us closely making notes on individuals, presumably for discussion about the progress we were making.

Needless to say, Eddie, myself, Ray and Paul threw ourselves wholeheartedly into every session, trying desperately to impress the coach and attempting to secure ourselves the chance of an apprenticeship with Everton. We were always thanked for our attendance at the end of each training session, but we were never given any feedback about how we had performed or given any indication as to our chances of being signed on. We did, however, have the consolation every week of having generous travelling expenses paid to us, which we grate-fully signed for and invariably spent before we had made our way back to Kirkby.

As our training sessions at Everton continued throughout the spring of 1969 and we continued to hear nothing about our chances, the four of us began to get a little discouraged. This was compounded by the fact that two of our team-mates, Steve Gregson and Phil Thompson had been offered a trial and an apprenticeship at Hull City and Liverpool respectively. I for one was beginning to lose a bit of hope.

Then one night, when I got back from training at Bellefield, my dad told me that he had had a visit from the Chief Scout from Burnley Football Club and that they wanted me, left-winger Eddie Avis and another of our Kirkby Boys players, centre-half Mick Quinn, to go there for a week's trial during the forthcoming school holiday. I couldn't wait to get round to Eddie and Mick's house to discuss our trial. For me, although I'd set my heart on an apprenticeship with Everton, if they weren't interested enough in me to offer me a contract, Burnley and their excellent youth set-up might provide the opportunity of a career in profes-sional football that I was desperate for.

The weeks before our trial flew by as we eagerly awaited the start of our week at Burnley, a club with a well established reputation for unearthing good schoolboy talent and developing it to produce a string of top flight players including Ralph Coates, Martin Dobson and the latest teen sensation, Leighton James, the speedy Welsh left-winger. This was a fact Eddie, myself and Mick discussed at length as we made the trip to Turf Moor. On arrival a taxi was provided for us to take us to the digs we would be staying in for the week. We were greeted by a kindly, rotund landlady who showed us to our rooms where we dropped our bags and got changed into our training gear after which the taxi took us on to the Burnley training ground just beyond the outskirts of the town.

In contrast to the enclosed suburban facilities at Bellefield, Burnley's training complex nestled in the rolling countryside at the foot of the Pennines just out of town making it appear bigger and more open. On arrival, we were met by one of the coaching staff who took us through to the Apprentices changing rooms where we were introduced to about ten of the Burnley youngsters and before long we had started the afternoon training session, which consisted of ball skills practice followed by a small sided game. After training, another taxi took us back to our digs where we enjoyed a hearty evening meal before watching some TV and an early night.

The format for the week was pretty much as it had been on the first day and was very similar to the sort of training Eddie and I had experienced at Bellefield, except that we were expected to help out with some of the apprentices' duties such as sweeping floors, preparing kit for the laundry and cleaning boots at the end of the day. We had very little to do with the first-team and other full-time pros, except for a couple of notable incidents, which provided a little insight into what life could be like as an apprentice professional footballer.

Firstly, on about the third day of training, we were getting changed in the apprentices changing room ready for the morning session when the calm atmosphere was shattered as the changing room door was kicked open and one of the younger full-time pros burst in and screamed at the top of his voice: "Where is he, the little bastard! My f******g shorts are still f******g damp!" Spotting the mortified apprentice who was responsible for his kit, the pro threw his shorts into the poor kid's face and continued his rant.

"Get them f******g dry – NOW!" And with that he dragged the youngster out of the room kicking him up the backside every other step, slamming the door behind him as he left the room. The stunned silence was broken by one of the older apprentices who stated, in a very matter of fact way,

"Don't worry about him, he's always moaning about something".

In spite of this reassurance, we Kirkby lads decided to give the pros a wide berth. However, another incident provided an additional eye-opener on the Friday when we were sweeping out the first-team dressing room after training had finished for the day just before lunchtime. We could hear a lot of shouting from along the corridor in the direction of the coaching staff changing rooms. As the raised voices neared where we were working, the first-teamers stopped dressing and waited to see what developed.

They were astonished to be met by the sight of a very tearful and distraught young Welshman, Leighton James as he flung open the door of the changing room and proceeded to slump onto one of the benches, head in hands, weeping uncontrollably, muttering oaths under his breath.

"What's the matter now Jamesey?" The question came from a half-dressed Martin Dobson.

"Not in the f******g team for tomorrow am I? The bastards!" And with that he continued to weep and swear intermittently.

Martin Dobson exchanged knowing glances with some of the other first-team players who soon finished dressing and left. We finished our duties as best we could and left Leighton James to his solitary misery.

These two incidents provided us with a brief, early glimpse of the harsh reality of life in the professional game. At the bottom, the apprentices being verbally and physically chastised and at the other end of the scale, the bitter disappointment and reaction of an up-and-coming first-teamer.

Naively, I assumed these incidents were isolated one-offs.

The week's trial culminated on the Saturday morning with a full trial match held between a mixture of apprentices and trialists who, like Eddie, Mick and myself, had attended evening coaching sessions or stayed for a week-long trial. Over the course of the week we felt we had acquitted ourselves quite well in training and in the trial match on the Saturday. As with our sessions at Everton, the coaches had not made any formal comments about our prospects. Instead, our dads had been invited across to see the trial match and afterwards to be guests of Burnley at their match at Turf Moor the same afternoon.

At the end of Burnley's match we were all invited into the plush surroundings of the Burnley F.C. boardroom where all manner of football dignitaries and club VIP's had assembled for their post-match social gathering. I stood with my dad on the periphery of the room trying not to look self-conscious when we were approached by the considerable figure of Mr. Bob Lord, the Burnley Chairman and owner, who said in his broad Lancashire twang:

"Now then Mr. Osborne, thank you for letting young Stanley come to Burnley for the week. The coaching staff have been impressed with him and, as you know, our scouts have been watching him for some time. I'd like him to sign for us as an apprentice professional and join the staff here at Burnley".

I was flattered and delighted and waited for my dad's response.

He paused for a moment and then replied, "Thank you for having him here and thanks for the offer but we are going to have to turn it down".

I looked at my dad as if he'd gone mad.

"Oh and why is that?" queried the rotund, ruddy-faced Chairman.

My Dad explained, "Stan's been training at Everton on Tuesdays and Thursdays and they've heard that he's been here at Burnley this week. Harry Cook, the Chief Scout and Jim Tansey, his assistant, turned up at our house today and they've said they are not leaving until I get him back to Kirkby to sign apprentice forms for Everton".

I expected Mr. Lord to be really disgruntled that his hospitality and offer of a contract had been rejected. However, he simply shrugged and said, "Well Everton are a big, big club. They are one of the biggest in the country and have a great youth set-up. And I know what keen Evertonians the family are. But here at Burnley, we have a really good record in bringing our youngsters through the ranks as well you know. Is there any chance of me persuading you to change your minds?"

An Agreement

An Agreement made the Eighth day of July 19 69 between

E. Catterick of Goodison Park

Liverpool in the COUNTY OF Lancashire

Manager

the Secretary of and acting pursuant to Resolution and Authority for and on behalf of the Everton FOOTBALL CLUB

of Goodison Park, Liverpool. 8. (hereinafter referred to as the Club)

of the one part and Stanley Osborne

of 21 Aldford Road, Southdene, Kirkby, Liverpool.

in the COUNTY OF Lancashire Apprentice Football Player

(hereinafter referred to as the Player) of the other part **Whereby** it is agreed as follows:—

1. The Player hereby agrees to play in an efficient manner and to the best of his ability for the Club.

2. The Player shall attend the Club's ground or any other place decided upon by the Club for the purposes of or in connection with his training as a Player pursuant to the instructions of the Secretary, Manager, or Trainer of the Club, or of such other person, or persons as the Club may appoint.

3. The Player shall do everything necessary to get and keep himself in the best possible condition so as to render the most efficient service to the Club, and will carry out all the training and other instructions of the Club through its representative officials.

4. The Player shall observe and be subject to all the Rules, Regulations and Bye-Laws of The Football Association, and any other Association, League, or Combination of which the Club shall be a member. And this Agreement shall be subject to any action which shall be taken by The Football Association under their Rules for the suspension or termination of the Football Season, and if any such suspension or termination shall be decided upon the payment of wages shall likewise be suspended or terminated, as the case may be.

5. The Player shall not engage in any business or live in any place which the Directors or Committee of the Club may deem unsuitable, provided that the Club shall, at the request of the Player or his Parent or Guardian, allow the Player to continue his further education or take up suitable vocational training.

6. If the Player shall be guilty of serious misconduct or breach of the disciplinary Rules of the Club, the Club may, on giving 14 days' notice to the said Player, or the Club may, on giving 28 days' notice to the said Player, on any reasonable grounds, terminate this Agreement and dispense with the services of the Player in pursuance of the Rules of all such Associations, Leagues,

10. In consideration of the observance by the said player of the terms, provisions and conditions of this Agreement, the said

E. Catterick on behalf of the Club hereby agrees that the said Club shall pay to the said Player the sum of £ 7 per week from 8th July 1969 to 13th September 1969

and £ 8 per week from 13th September 1969

to 13th September 1970 and £ 10 per week from 13th September 1970 to 13th September 1971

and £ per week from

to and £ per week from

to

11. This Agreement (subject to the Rules of The Football Association) shall cease and determine on 13th September 1971 unless the same shall have been previously determined in accordance with the provisions hereinbefore set forth.

Fill in any other provisions required

As Witness the hands of the said parties the day and year first aforesaid

Signed by the said E. Catterick

and

Stanley Osborne S. Osborne (Player)

In the presence of the Parent or Guardian of the Player

(Signature) E. K. Osborne H. Catterick (Secretary) (Manager)

(Occupation) Aircraft Driver

(Address) 21 Aldford Road,
Southdene, Kirkby, Liverpool.

But he could see by our reactions that there was little point in pursuing the question and in a resigned tone, he wished me all the best with my football before returning to group of Director-types at the bar. Sadly, there was to be no offer of contracts from Burnley for Eddie and Mick who returned home disappointed.

Listening to my dad explain about Harry Cook's surprise visit to our house had the hairs standing up on the back of my neck. I thought I had missed my chance at Everton because they had never even mentioned the possibility of signing when I was training at Bellefield on so many occasions. It was like a dream. I was stunned and could hardly speak as we made our way back over the Pennines from Burnley to Kirkby. It was as though my dreams had been answered.

When we arrived back at 21 Aldford Road, Southdene, the large, shiny car that had been parked outside our house for a few hours was attracting inquisitive stares from the neighbours. Once inside, I remember vividly the conversation between my dad and Harry Cook:

Harry Cook: I'll be quite straightforward with you Mr. Osborne. We want to sign Stan because we consider him to be one of the finest schoolboy centre forward prospects in the country at the moment. We've had our scouts watching him all season with Kirkby Boys. His goal scoring speaks for itself and at Everton we only accept the best. We want him as an apprentice and with our coaching and development and his hard work and dedication we think he has a chance of making the grade. Have you got any questions?

Dad: Yes, will he be allowed to continue with his studies if he signs?

Harry Cook: Yes, Mr. Osborne. If Stan signs for Everton on Apprentice Professional forms, under F.A. rules, we have to provide what are known as 'alternative education and training facilities'.

Dad: What exactly does that mean?

Harry Cook: I know Stan is in the middle of his 'O' Level exam courses at Brookfield at the moment, but he can be released to attend Childwall Hall County College on Mondays instead of training at Bellefield. Peter Scott already goes there and Stan knows him from Kirkby Boys last year.

Dad: But won't that put him at a disadvantage with not training on Mondays?

Harry Cook: No, none of the apprentices train on Mondays. The ones who don't go to college to study, spend the day as trainee mechanics at a centre on the Kirkby Industrial Estate. It's so that if they weren't to make the grade as professional footballers, they'll have something to fall back on.

Dad: OK. What about wages?

Harry Cook: Everton pay the standard F.A. rate for Apprentice Professionals, which is £7.00 a week in the first year. This rises to £8.00 in the second year and then £10.00 in the final year. Apprentices also receive £1.00 win bonus or 50p draw bonus whoever they play for at the club. Then, if we sign an apprentice as a full-time pro, we offer a one year contract of £18.00 per week with the option of a second year. Newly signed professionals also receive a £250 signing on fee.

Throughout this conversation all I could do was wish my dad would just shut up and let me sign the forms. Finally, my dad turned to me and said, "Well son, it's up to you. What do you want to do?"

Precisely ten seconds later and with my mum and dad looking on proudly, I signed two sets of apprentice professional forms and was officially the newest recruit of Everton Football Club.

Mr. Cook said that he would have to take the forms for Harry Catterick to sign on behalf of the club and that I would receive a copy of the contract afterwards. Jim Tansey then produced a plastic-spined booklet from his briefcase and handed it to me. The cover depicted the silhouette a young Everton player heading a ball and was titled simply, 'Everton & You'. He explained that the booklet was produced for new apprentices to give them an insight into what they could expect from an apprenticeship at Everton Football Club before they actually started their contracts.

As they were leaving, Harry Cook casually stated, "By the way, you're not the only one from Kirkby Boys we've given one of those booklets to. You're going to have company on the bus to Bellefield when you start. We've signed Ray Pritchard and we're interested in Paul McEwan as well! And Ronny Goodlass and Ian Bacon from Liverpool Boys and Mick Buckley from Manchester Boys."

Having played against Mick Buckley once and three times against Ronny Goodlass that season and knowing they, along with my team-mate Ray Pritchard were England Schoolboy Internationals brought home to me the standard of players Everton had secured as apprentices – and that I was one of them! As we saw Mr. Cook and Mr. Tansey to the door, my chest was bursting with pride and excitement and as they drove off all I wanted to do was scream out to everyone in the street that I was a real life, truly signed-on, paid to play football, royal blue wearing Everton footballer. I could barely contain myself and couldn't wait to get back to school and tell all my mates what had happened.

Word of our signing for Everton spread like wildfire amongst the close knit Kirkby community via the schools, pubs and social clubs. It also transpired that at roughly the same time, two other Kirkby Boys had signed contracts with professional clubs. Phil Thompson had signed as an apprentice for Liverpool FC and Steve Gregson for Hull City. Along with us three at Everton, that amounted to quite a crop of talent produced that year from an overspill town on the outskirts of Liverpool.

In the time before I started at Everton, I forget how many times I read the booklet that Jim Tansey gave me from cover to cover. It was my constant companion and I think I memorised virtually every word it contained, including a foreword from the then Chairman, Jack Sharp and explanations about the role of Harry Catterick and his coaching staff. It went on to illustrate in detail the training facilities at Bellefield, the training methods, diet and medical care and backup available and the standard of football competition apprentices could expect to play in.

All of this information was depicted in action photographs of former apprentices, many of whom had now progressed and still played for the club as full-time professionals. Finally, if everything it mentioned previously wasn't enough to inspire a youngster, 'Everton & You' laid out the potential rewards to be gained through a successful career at a club like Everton, summarising them by stating that a figure of around £4,000 a year might be achieved by a successful first-team player. This was a fact wonderfully illustrated by a photograph of one of my heroes, Colin Harvey, emerging from his Jaguar resplendent in a suit and trilby.

This inspirational publication summarised the position I found myself in having signed for the club in a section at the end, appropriately opposite a picture of the current first-team squad:

'You have read all that we can tell you of what your life would be like as a football apprentice with Everton. Your training will be as good as any and better than most. And you will be on the staff of a Club that will never be content to be 'just another League Club', but one which intends to reach – and stay on – the highest peaks of football fame. Yours is an opportunity which comes very rarely, and then only to a fortunate few'.

And fortunate was exactly how I felt as I looked forward to starting my apprenticeship at Everton. The thought of actually being paid to play the sport I lived, ate and breathed for made me feel euphoric enough, but added to that, the prospect of rubbing shoulders and playing alongside the likes of Alan Ball, Brian Labone, Joe Royle, Howard Kendall and Colin Harvey who, only a few short months earlier, I had been supporting from the Gwladys Street end at Goodison Park was simply surreal.

'Everton & You' had told me everything that the club could tell me about life as an apprentice. Whether or not that was everything I needed to know was something I wouldn't find out until I actually pulled on my boots for the first time as an Everton player in July 1969.

* * * *

Before I officially left school, there was one formality that I wasn't looking forward to. That was making an appointment to see Mr. Bury, the Head Teacher of my school, Brookfield.

Mr. Bury was highly regarded and respected within the community in our area, Southdene and in the wider community in Kirkby. He had been appointed as Head when the school opened in the 1950's and had built the school's reputation as it had grown to a massive institution with approaching 2000 pupils and over a hundred staff as more and more families arrived from Liverpool following the slum clearance programme, which was designed to rid the city of the worst of its overcrowded and dilapidated housing stock in the Everton and Scotland Road areas. Brookfield Comprehensive was no Eton or Harrow, but pupils were effectively streamed so that they were able to access a curriculum, which suited their aptitudes and abilities. The more academic students were taught to gear up for the 'O' and 'A' Level exam courses, with more technically minded pupils following other additional subjects such as technical drawing. Other more practical subjects were also catered for including metalwork, woodwork and motor mechanics.

Make no bones about it, Brookfield was a tough school and pupils and staff alike had to have their wits about them to survive and progress. I and many of my schoolmates were no strangers to corporal punishment, which was meted out regularly when the occasion and behaviour warranted. But this was the 1960's and there was no hue and cry about physical punishment in schools. We accepted our punishment, without complaint, in the knowledge that it was invariably administered justly and fairly and on the basis that it was preferable to what we might expect as punishment if word of our more serious breaches of school discipline ever reached home.

Mr. Bury certainly ran a well-disciplined school and we were fortunate to be taught by some truly inspirational teachers, not least of whom taught in the PE Department. Alan Bonner as Head of Department and John Crompton, an American athletics coach who seemed to run round in bare feet, indoors and out, whatever the weather and inspired many of us to take up track and field events. Then there was Bob Downing, who started at the school as a newly qualified teacher at the time we transferred to Brookfield from primary school. Bob was an awesome character who was to eventually spend the whole of his career at the school. Through his dedication, support and encouragement he enabled me and countless kids like me to take up and enjoy the sport of their choice and progress to local, county and international level. A superb coach who gave generously and freely of his time, Bob was the driving force behind the consistently high standards achieved in football at the school.

As Headteacher, Mr. Bury was a keen advocate of sport and took great pleasure in announcing any notable achievements gained on the sports field during his morning assemblies. However, his burning ambition was to see the academic standards in the school improve and many was the time in assemblies that he cautioned us about the pitfalls that existed for would-be footballers stressing the over-riding importance of gaining a decent education and qualifications.

So it was with a heavy heart that I sat in the hushed corridor outside Mr. Bury's office having asked his secretary if he could spare me a moment. Out of the glass panelled door at the end, I could see the busy hubbub of pupils and staff milling about between lessons and it dawned on me that before long I would be leaving the security of life as a schoolboy to face the challenges of the adult world.

"I think I know why you want to see me", Mr. Bury said looking over the top of his glasses from behind his huge desk, as I settled into the chair opposite him. He continued, "I had a call this morning from Mr. Cook, the chief scout at Everton and he informs me that you have signed an apprentice professional contract and that you will be leaving us.

"Yes, that's why I wanted to see you, to ask for permission to leave school before the end of term so I can start training with Everton", I replied. Remembering his warnings about the pitfalls of being a footballer and hearing the disapproving tone of his voice, I was sort of expecting what he said next.

"Stanley, you are in the top sets for all your 'O' Level courses and have taken your English exam a year early and passed with flying colours and you're expected to sit the rest of your exams at the end of next year before going into the Sixth Form for your 'A' Level courses. I would expect you to go on to university and you are prepared to throw that chance away in the hope of making a living out of football?" He gave me a Headmasterly frown as he waited for my reply.

"It's what I've always wanted to do. I've dreamed of getting this chance with Everton", I said, choking back the emotion as I spoke.

Mr. Bury looked at me thoughtfully for a few moments, then leaned forward and linked his fingers in front of him as they rested on his desk.

"Look, I know it's your dream. And thousands of kids like you have had that dream and for most of them it's the only chance they'll get. But you have a choice. You've got other abilities, not only the ones in your feet. If you were my son, I'd make you stay at school to finish your 'O' Levels then let you leave to play football."

He paused for a moment and in a resigned tone added, " But you're not my son and I've spoken to your parents too and they want you to leave school – so that's the end of the matter".

He got up from behind his desk and offered me his hand saying, "I wish you all the best with your football, and I hope to see you playing at Goodison Park one day, but promise me one thing. Promise me you will continue with your studies so that if it doesn't work out for you for some reason, you'll have something to fall back on".

I made that promise and left Mr. Bury's office knowing I had his blessing but also that I had a lot to live up to, in his eyes at least.

* * * *

At home, my mum and dad were waiting and could hardly contain their joy when I told them that Mr. Bury had given permission for me to leave school in a couple of weeks to start training with Everton as an apprentice professional. This was an opportunity the family could only have dreamed of for one of their brood, when we were moved lock, stock and barrel to Kirkby new town from our tiny terraced house in Samuel Street, Everton during the early 1950's, having received a notice that ours was one of the thousands earmarked for demolition.

The phrase extended family could have been coined to describe us back then, when the Osborne's were indeed an extended family living throughout the Everton Valley and Scotland Road area of Liverpool. My dad Ted was the third eldest of thirteen Osborne children and my mum, Elsie senior, one of six children in the Cummings family. Large numbers of children in families was not unusual or uncommon in Liverpool at the time. I was the youngest of the six children in our household and was one of 57 cousins that my eldest sister Elsie once calculated lived within a square mile or so of the famous St George's Church which stands as a prominent landmark on the brow of St Domingo Road, near Everton Library.

We joined the exodus of over 100,000 people from Everton, and the Kirkdale and Scotland Road areas, who were promised modern housing, healthier living conditions, better schools, employment opportunities on the Kirkby Industrial Estate and state of the art amenities and leisure facilities. This, the town planners told us, was to be a new start away from the post war squalor that existed within the crumbling, neglected, tightly packed terraced streets that ran down from St. Domingo Road and Heyworth Street to

Netherfield Road and on to Scotland Road at the bottom of Everton Valley. It was to be an end, they said, to the overcrowded, insanitary conditions and deliverance to a better, healthier life beyond the city limits.

But if you ask anyone who grew up in Kirkby in the 50's and 60's, they will probably tell you that the reality was very different. The housing was modern but basic and in many cases poor quality. Most of the schools were still being built around us. (Rushey Hey Junior School in Southdene was even housed in a defunct army barracks). When we first arrived, shops were virtually non-existent and leisure facilities were just a distant dream.

In spite of the best efforts of the new arrivals to recreate the close-knit community infrastructure from their city roots, the social consequences of such poorly planned development were predictable. However unjustly, in the eyes of many external observers the Kirkby where we grew up, rather than being a model of good practice for urban resettlement that we were promised, became synonymous with unemployment, poverty and crime.

This was a picture painted and reinforced by TV series such as 'Z Cars', but this wasn't entirely accurate. Yes, the housing estates were huge and anonymous with row after row of pebble-dashed terraced houses interspersed with flats, maisonettes and high-rise blocks resulting in the environment in Kirkby being harsh, but we were used to that when we were living in Everton. But that did not prevent the new Kirkby residents trying to recreate the sense of community and camaraderie which existed for them previously, being re-established and in spite of the difficulties we experienced, a feeling of optimism and real hope about the future still prevailed.

We were allocated a three bedroomed terraced house in Aldford Road, in Southdene, the first area of Kirkby to be developed and settled. My two sisters Elsie and Jean weren't there for long before they were married. Elsie and her husband Billy moved to Aintree and Jean and her husband Geoff eventually settled in Suffolk having moved there with his job as an accountant. That left eldest son Eddie, David, Alan and myself at home and doing most of our schooling at Cherryfield Infant and Junior School and Brookfield Comp and our growing up on the streets of Kirkby.

By the time I was seeing out my last few weeks at school prior to joining Everton my dad had retired early on medical grounds from his long distance lorry driving job, which he had done for many years at J. Bibby and Son on Vauxhall Road in Liverpool. As well as looking after her brood, my mum was also a cleaner at Brookfield School. Eldest brother Eddie was working in the office at J. Bibby and Son but he left to pursue his love of climbing, walking and the outdoors, working for the Forestry Commission as a woodman in North Wales. Meanwhile Alan had been working for a year or so on the production line at Fords Halewood plant in Speke.

That left David, who was severely disabled due to suffering cerebral palsy. Although he wore callipers and his speech was slow, he had a zest for life, loved music and enjoyed his days at the Mercer Vale Training Centre in West

Vale, just across town from us. Because I was the only member of the household who wasn't working, one of my jobs was to ensure that David was helped to board the coach to Mercer Vale every morning before I went to school, and be there to help him back unsteadily into the house (football commitments allowing) when the coach brought him home in the evening.

Because of Dave's disabilities, this was always a task I performed with a great deal of self-consciousness as it always attracted inquisitive stares from people who happened to be walking past. However, once they had satisfied their curiosity, they usually passed without comment unless it was, "Hi Dave" or, "Hi Stan".

But there was one older kid who lived in the flats opposites our house, who couldn't help but make derogatory or demeaning and insulting remarks if ever he happened to be passing at the time. Something along the lines of, "Oh here comes spastic legs" or "Watch out for the cripple" usually delivered with a sneering arrogance, which produced embarrassed amusement amongst the three or so cronies who accompanied him wherever he went.

The insults didn't bother Dave, who ignored them and just shouted, "Go away! Don't like yer!"

But it really got me fuming every time it happened. I didn't tell anyone what was going on but decided there would be a place and a time when I would be able to get even for the insults he was subjecting me and Dave to. The opportunity to do just that came sooner than I expected.

* * * *

With only a matter of weeks to go before I left school to start training alongside my Kirkby Boys team-mates at Everton, my mind was fully focused on maintaining my fitness and getting into the best shape possible. Typically, Bob Downing encouraged me to use the weights in the gym at Brookfield and even arranged a fitness regime involving interval training runs around the school playing fields and some intensive work on key skills like heading, passing, ball control, shooting and dribbling. It was after one of these sessions, when a number of lads were changing that we noticed some leaflets, which had been circulated to the PE Departments of the Kirkby Schools inviting any boys who were interested in joining the Kirkby Amateur Boxing Club to go along to their headquarters for a trial sparring session.

The Boxing Club was founded in West Vale and was housed in a small gym at the rear of the stand at Kirkby Stadium on Valley Road adjacent to the Kirkby exit slip road off the M57. It was a thriving club, which had a growing reputation in view of the fact that John Conteh was a member before he went on to win the gold medal at light heavyweight at the 1967 Commonwealth Games and was making rapid progress towards a world title fight as a pro. Needless to say there was a great deal of interest in the sparring sessions, including myself and a few of my mates.

I mentioned to my dad about the sessions at the boxing club so he and a few of the other dads came along to see how we did. When we arrived at the gym, fully expecting to be the next John Conteh, the evening got off to quite a chaotic start with boys of different ages and sizes being shown the rudiments of stance, guard and sparring. We joined in and were soon gliding around the gym floating like butterflies and stinging like bees – or so we thought, while younger boys were gloved up and paired up for mini-bouts in the boxing ring.

As the evening progressed, different age groups had their mini bouts. Then an announcement went up, "Any 16-year-olds ready?"

I was amazed to see the first one up in the ring was none other than the older lad from our street who was giving myself and our Dave all the abuse when I was collecting him from his coach. Typically, he was prancing around the ring doing the 'Ali Shuffle' raising his hand above his head occasionally and announcing, "I am The Greatest, I am The Greatest!" much to the amusement of his mates and the annoyance of everyone else.

"Any more?" the organiser yelled above the hubbub.

This was the opportunity to get even that I had been waiting for. Straight away I shouted, "Yes, I'll have a go", and in a flash I was under the ropes and being gloved up. I noticed by dad at the ringside. He tapped me on the arm and asked, "Are you sure – he's 16, they're doing the 15 year olds later?"

I smiled and said, "Oh yes, I'm sure".

This was more than just a sparring match to me. This was my chance to wipe the sneer off that bully's face. This was my chance to get even for all the insults.

As we faced each other in the middle of the ring, the referee said, "It's just a 3 minute sparring session. Don't go mad!"

I can still picture the bully's sneer as we touched gloves before the bout and he jutted his chin towards me and said, "Where's your cripple brother tonight?"

Then the bell sounded.

I remember the first two or three punches wiping the sneer off my opponents face and the blood running from his nose but the rest of the contest was just a blur until I felt a strong grip on my shoulders pulling me away from him. The referee's words were ringing in my ears, "Leave him, leave him, he's had enough!"

When the red mist had dispersed from my head slightly, I could see the bully boy lying on the canvas, blood smeared across his face. As they helped him out of the ring I leaned over him and as he cowered away from me, I whispered, "Don't call my brother a spastic or a cripple again".

As I was climbing out of the ring, the organiser called over, "Hang on a minute, we want to have another look at you".

So I sat down on the stool in my corner of the ring as they ushered in another 'opponent', who I recognised immediately as one of the Bean family from West Vale. The Bean family were as equally well known as John Conteh and his family were in Kirkby at the time and, needless to say, they were not to be trifled with.

However, emboldened by my success in my first 'bout', it was with some confidence that I squared up to Mr. Bean waiting for the bell to sound. The next thing I remember was looking up at the lights as I lay on my back with the referee leaning over me asking if I was OK. This process of squaring up to Mr. Bean and immediately being knocked senseless onto the canvas was repeated twice more in quick succession. The third time I sat up with my head still spinning and looked to the side of the ring to see my dad peering at me from between the ropes. I stared vacantly back at him looking for inspiration – it wasn't long in coming.

"You better get out of there before you get a cauliflower arse", he said dryly.

I didn't need any further guidance and my brief boxing career ended there and then, thankfully, as quickly as it had begun.

On the way home my dad broke the silence as we walked back across Brookfield school fields towards Aldford Road.

"That first lad you boxed against, you really had a go at him didn't you? Had he upset you or something?"

I didn't say anything at first but then replied,

"He said some things about our Dave, Dad. You know, nasty things about him being handicapped and that".

"Oh", my dad said with a smile, "I don't think he'll be saying any more after tonight".

****

As the memory of my brief flirtation with boxing quickly receded, my anticipation of starting as a new recruit at Everton Football Club came even more sharply into focus in the days before I started my apprenticeship. Our season with Kirkby Boys had been a huge success and my confidence as a free scoring centre forward should have been high. But my mind was full of questions that my trial at Burnley couldn't answer and it didn't matter how many times I read 'Everton & You', I was still anxious about what to expect once I started at Everton as a player. What would the other apprentices be like? What would full-time training be like? How long would we train? Would we train with the full-time pros or the first-team sometimes? What happens if you get injured? Who would our trainer/coach be? What other duties would we have? These were just some of the questions that were swimming around in my head.

My dad could only suggest that I worked as hard as I could and listen to what I was told to do and do it to the best of my ability. Bob Downing told me to prepare for a very competitive environment that would test any schoolboy footballer's talents to the limit.

In the end I made my mind up that there was only one way to find the answers to these questions and that was to walk into training at Bellefield for the first time, get my boots on and get stuck in!

JULY 1969
NEW
ARRIVALS

When I caught the 15D bus from opposite the shops at the bottom of Broad Lane in Southdene, I was full of anticipation about what my first day at Everton would have in store. I knew by then that Ray Pritchard and Paul McEwan, my Kirkby Boys team-mates would be joining me. Articles in the Liverpool Echo had also named Ronny Goodlass and Ian Bacon (Liverpool Boys), Mick Buckley (Manchester Boys) and Peter Whitwood (Essex Boys) as players who would be starting at Everton as apprentices at the same time. Having played against Ronny, Ian and Mick as outstanding schoolboys the previous season, I was eager to get to know them.

Fortunately, I met Ray on the same bus, he having caught it earlier on its route in Northwood. After the journey, changing buses at Norris Green, the long walk up the driveway at Bellefield was a strange, almost eerie experience. I expected it to be a hive of activity with training sessions and 5-a-side matches to be under way. Instead there was nobody to be seen until we spotted two track-suited youngsters with a tin of white paint and a couple paint brushes squatting down earnestly engaged in giving some five-a-side goalposts a fresh coat of gloss. I recognised them immediately as, now ex-Liverpool Schoolboys, Ronny Goodlass and Ian Bacon.

Ronny spotted us first and said, "Alright lads. Glad you're here we could do with a bit of help. There's another two pairs of these goalposts to paint!"

"Yeah, we'll give you hand when we've got our kit organised", I replied.

Ian Bacon said, "OK but we've got to go in soon because we're being introduced to the new coach, Stewart Imlach this morning so we'll see you in the players' lounge later".

We made our way inside to be met by Joe, the Bellefield caretaker-cum-handyman. A short, dapper man in his 60's with a shock of white hair and enormous owl-like horn-rimmed glasses, it was easy to see why he'd acquired the nickname 'Joe 90'. He showed us up into the players' lounge where we waited to meet our new coach. Ronny and Ian soon followed as the rest of the apprentices arrived having broken off from whatever their tasks for the morning were. The new apprentices were joined by eight second-year apprentices and the 14 of us waited a little self-consciously for the arrival of Stewart Imlach. It appeared from the comments made before he arrived, that nobody had actually met Stewart Imlach, but his pedigree as a Scottish International and winger for Nottingham Forest was mentioned.

At this point the air of anticipation wasn't exactly helped when somebody released the loudest and foulest smelling fart imaginable a matter of seconds before Stewart Imlach entered the room to meet his new charges for the first time. Consequently, instead of being met by a group of highly motivated apprentices waiting to hang on his every word, he was met by a group of youths rolling about laughing and gasping for air – not the best start with a new coach!

In spite of this indiscretion, Mr. Imlach kept his composure and after directing someone to open a few windows, set about introducing himself explaining that he would be in charge of the 'B' Team playing in the Lancashire League, whilst Tommy Casey, a former Northern Ireland international, would be running the 'A' Team in their Lancashire League division. Arthur Proudler would continue as Reserve team coach for the Central League team with Wilf Dixon in charge of the first-team. This information was delivered by Mr. Imlach in a clipped, precise Scottish twang, and was absorbed eagerly by myself and the other apprentices as he gave each of us the once over with darting hawk-like eyes as he paced the players' lounge dressed in his brand new blue canvas drill tracksuit and gleaming white Dunlop Green Flash trainers. He was a short impish man in his mid to late thirties with short, cropped hair and a thin wiry build and willowy, slightly bowed legs.

After his brief introduction, he stated that he had already been told a little bit about the new apprentices including myself and asked the older, second-year apprentices to introduce themselves. The next ten minutes or so were spent with the older lads giving us all a brief summary of themselves as follows:

Peter Scott (full back) and Keith Williams (goalkeeper) – ex Kirkby Boys, John (Tigsy) Smith (midfield), Alan Wilson (centre forward) and Joe Moran (midfield) – ex Liverpool Boys, Les Ormerod (full back) – ex Manchester Boys, Davey Graham (full back)– ex Sefton Boys and finally Bobby Armstrong (full back) – ex Maghull Boys. We learned that Les was previously England Schoolboys captain and that John Smith had also been capped the previous year. Most of them had progressed from the 'B' Team to the 'A' Team in their first year at Everton and Peter Scott had also played for the Reserves. If we didn't realise it before this meeting, it became clear very quickly to me and the other new recruits that we had a lot of competition even from within the apprentices, never mind the pros at the club.

Once he was satisfied that he had familiarised himself fully with the assembled apprentice ranks, myself and Ray were told to remain whilst the rest of the lads were re-assigned to their tasks around the grounds and in the changing rooms. We were then escorted by Stewart downstairs to the Kit Room where we were to be kitted out 'National Service' style with our requisite training gear.

The Kit Room was a small fairly cramped area, which doubled as a drying room where kit and towels were dried between training stints ready for subsequent sessions. It was dominated by two industrial sized driers, which hummed and droned away as a jumble of multi-coloured kits somersaulted rhythmically inside their chrome drums.

Stewart unlocked and slid open the doors of the kit cupboards, which were to the left of the entrance into the Kit Room. They were stacked out neatly with the same brand new blue canvas drill tracksuits that Stewart was wearing as well as a variety of brand new assorted striped rugby jerseys, which I noticed had 'Jack Sharp' labels in. Jack Sharp owned the famous sports equipment shop in Liverpool and was Chairman and prominent member of the board at Everton. Similarly, brand new socks, shorts and royal blue towels were also waiting to be allocated. I was quite looking forward to having my set of pristine new training gear ready to grace the lavish facilities waiting outside on the lush green Bellefield grass.

Then reality hit as Stewart reached down below the bottom shelf and produced a tatty cardboard box full of threadbare, used and worn kit.

"Sort yourselves out from that lot. I'll be back in a minute with the key to the boot cupboard", he said over his shoulder as he left the Kit Room.

Ray and I didn't speak; we just looked at each other, then rummaged through the jumble of old rugby shirts, socks and shorts, eventually finding enough items of kit that weren't too badly holed to make up a full set each, which we folded neatly and waited for Mr. Imlach to return. It was obvious the other apprentices had been there before us and helped themselves to the best of what was in the box – first come first served I supposed ruefully.

Stewart returned whistling jauntily with the boot cupboard key dangling from his fingers with which he unlocked the cupboard. Boxes of top of the range Adidas '2000' boots of various sizes adorned the shelves along with Adidas 'Samba' leather trainers. However, as with the kit, we soon realised such quality gear was not for the likes of us apprentices. Stewart slid a second door open to reveal the lower quality Adidas 'Santiago' boots and Dunlop Green Flash white canvas training pumps to which we were allocated a pair each. Not what we would have liked, but at least they were new!

Stewart then supervised us as we marked our own initials on each item of kit using a stencil and indelible black shoe dye. After changing into our 'new' training kits we were then teamed up with the other apprentices who were already engaged in painting goalposts, wheel barrowing soil around the grounds or other cleaning and maintenance tasks, which continued after a short lunch break for cottage pie upstairs in the canteen. This was to be our routine for the first week or so at an eerily quiet Bellefield with no sign of the first-team or other pros – just the apprentices and the ground staff involved in all duties – other than football. I wondered when we would actually do some training and couldn't wait to be immersed in the ways of Everton's famous School of Science.

Instead, if they wanted to ensure that their new apprentices quickly forgot their status as star schoolboy footballers, allocating them old, worn out kit and having them mop floors, clean toilets, shovel soil and paint goalposts for a week certainly worked. We were at the bottom of the pecking order – and we knew it! All good character building stuff.

Most of the ground work done by the apprentices was supervised by Head Groundsman, Dougie Rose and his assistant Sid McGuiness. Dougie was a tall powerfully built man of about 55 who had huge bucket-like hands and was usually accompanied by his faithful Labrador. Sid was a short, round man of similar age and a ruddy, weather beaten complexion and was usually accompanied by the latest copy of a girlie magazine such as Playboy or Parade. They were not men to be trifled with and did their own bit to knock any sense of celebrity out of our thoughts.

But they were a fund of anecdotes and jokes, which used to lighten the load during some of the more laborious work. They also kept us informed about the gossip surrounding the first-team and some of the possible signings for Everton. I sometimes got the feeling that they heard transfer news before the trainers or the manager. In fact it was Sid who told us when the pros and first-team squad were due back to start pre-season training, which was about two weeks after the apprentices started back.

Prior to the arrival of the first-team and other pros for the start of the pre-season training regime, the coaching staff allocated the apprentices to their responsibilities regarding who looked after which pros dressing room. This included being responsible for preparing the training kit and boots before and after each session, cleaning the dressing room and shower areas as well as any other incidental tasks required by the pros. Again there was a pecking order, with the senior apprentices looking after the Trainers/Managers room and the first-team changing room. The reserves and junior professionals were allocated to the younger apprentices.

Once the decision about where the apprentices were allocated was taken, there was a huge amount of preparation to be done to ensure that the pros had all their kit and footwear ready. All shirts, shorts, socks, towels and boots had to be stencilled with each of the pro's squad number for easy identification and sorting when kit arrived back from the laundry at Goodison Park or was being dried after training sessions. Match and practice balls had to be inflated, ready for training and the finishing touches to all the external fixtures and equipment completed. Predictably, I was allocated to the junior pros changing room along with Paul McEwan, Ray Pritchard and Peter Whitwood. We were also allocated specific pros, usually four each, whose kit was our individual responsibility. From what the older lads said, some of the pros were easily pleased while some of them were never pleased whatever you did. That was something I would find out soon enough.

Finally, with all the preparation done and with Bellefield shining like the proverbial new pin, on the eve of the start of pre-season training for the 1969-1970 season, the organisation of the 32 full-time professionals and 14 full-time apprentices and coaching staff for Everton Football Club looked like this:- Manager and Coaches Changing Room: Harry Catterick, Wilf Dixon, Arthur Proudler, Tommy Casey, Stewart Imlach. (Apprentices – Peter Scott, Les Ormrod)

First-team Changing Room: Sandy Brown, Johnny Morrissey, Gordon West, Tommy Wright, Brian Labone, Alan Ball, John Hurst, Colin Harvey, Howard Kendall, Joe Royle, Jimmy Husband. (Apprentices – Alan Wilson, John Smith, Joe Moran, Davey Graham)

Reserves Changing Room: Harry Bennett, Geoff Barnett, Frank D'Arcy, Roger Kenyon, Archie Styles, Terry Darracott, Gerry Humphreys, Tommy Jackson, Terry Owen, Steve Melledew, Andy Rankin. (Apprentices – Bobby Armstrong, Ronny Goodlass, Ian Bacon, Keith Williams)

Junior Professional's Changing Room: Alec Clark, Bryn Jones, David Johnson, Tommy Hughes, Mick Lyons, Gary Jones, Mike Westburgh, Dave Turner, Steve Seargeant, Billy Brindle, Billy Kenny. (Apprentices – Stan Osborne, Paul McEwan, Ray Pritchard, Mick Buckley, Peter Whitwood)

Apprentices Changing Room: Peter Scott, Les Ormrod, John Smith, Alan Wilson, Joe Moran, Mick Buckley, Keith Williams, Bobby Armstrong, Davey Graham, Ronny Goodlass, Ian Bacon, Stan Osborne, Ray Pritchard, Paul McEwan, Peter Whitwood.

* * * * * *

It wasn't until the first-team players started back at Bellefield for pre-season training that it fully dawned on me that I had actually arrived at Everton. As the apprentices went about their early morning duties, we would watch as the cars arrive and a who's who of Everton players strolled towards the dressing room entrance looking bronzed and relaxed after their summer breaks in far off foreign climes. Alan Ball parked his gleaming white Sunbeam Alpine sports car and casually called over to some of the older apprentices, "Alright lads, had a good break?

Or Howard Kendall would get out of his blue Jag and be joking with Joe Royle as they walked across the car park. One after the other; Brian Labone, Gordon West, Johnny Morrissey, Jimmy Husband – all heroes of mine who only a few short months earlier, I had been paying to watch at Goodison Park and now I was here rubbing shoulders with them. It was hard not to be intimidated or overawed.

As we got to know them and they began to recognise us as new apprentices when we were fetching and carrying for them, the first-team players were friendly enough. Obviously, as with any workplace, there were the initiation ceremonies and ritual piss-taking. For example, there were always first-team squad photographs and other paraphernalia and merchandising, which was left out in the players' lounge on a daily basis ready for the players to autograph. It was once insisted, as a matter of great urgency, that I take a squad photograph up to the Manager's Office for Mr. Catterick to sign his autograph on when they knew he was in the middle of an important meeting with the press. This I did with naïve enthusiasm only to be sent away with a flea in my ear for daring to interrupt! All pretty light-hearted stuff reflecting the fact that established first-teamers were comfortable in the fact that we apprentices were no real threat to them.

With the reserves and especially the younger professionals though, things were often different. Some of the piss-taking was more serious and bordered on bullying. De-bagging and having to run the gauntlet of wet towels being flicked at you or being dumped fully clothed into the cold plunge baths for minor oversights or misdemeanours was not uncommon and was treated as part and parcel of the young apprentices' lot. We were warned though by the older lads that a 'Court Case' was to be avoided at all costs. This was usually a hastily arranged 'kangaroo court' in the younger professional's dressing room to hold a 'trial' of one of the apprentices for serious offences such as being overly keen to curry favour with the coaching staff or getting above your station or being 'big time'. They stopped short of telling us what the punishment for inevitably being found 'guilty' was, but it was clearly unlikely to be pleasant. This was something we would find out soon enough.

So with weeks of ground staff duties out of the way and with a keen sense of anticipation about when another piss-take was to happen and with wary eye on the younger professionals, pre-season training finally got under way. But this wasn't training as we had expected it to be.

On that first Monday, the whole of the playing staff, from the first-team squad right down to the humble apprentices were told to assemble in trainers (or pumps if you were an apprentice) outside the main dressing room block. Here we were paired up and organised into a long phalanx of players with the first-team at the front followed, in pecking order, by the reserve squad, then young pros with the apprentices bringing up the rear. The training staff were spaced out at regular intervals to the side of the players, each keeping a watchful eye on their squads as we proceeded to lap the grounds of Bellefield in what can only be described as a forced march.

Every so often we would stop, break off into groups and do a series of stretching exercises for achilles tendons, calf muscles, hamstrings and quadriceps. Alternately we also broke off for abdominal work, sit-ups, press-ups or squat thrusts. This continued for about an hour and a half continuously, throughout which time the coaches barked out instructions and forced the pace at which we marched while Wilf Dixon informed us that this form of 'warm up' was essential to prevent muscle tears and tendon strains. We were also told to expect this for at least a week and that we wouldn't be seeing a football for a good while yet!

This laborious process was repeated after a lunch break for about another hour and a half, by which time every muscle in my body was throbbing and aching – likewise with the rest of the apprentices. I didn't think it was possible for training to be so strenuous without even running!

Wilf Dixon and the other coaches were true to their word – this tedious and unrelenting regime of marching interspersed with stretches and strengthening exercises was maintained for the whole of the first week of training. Understandably rumblings of discontent at the boring and repetitive nature of the training began to emerge from within the ranks. However any complaints were dealt with ruthlessly by ordering the complainant to do additional sit-ups or press-ups on the spot.

Throughout this first week, Harry Catterick remained a shadowy figure, remaining aloof and only being seen in person arriving or leaving the training ground in his gleaming white Rover 3500. However he was often seen at one of the upstairs windows of his office observing the massed training regime with his steely glare. This frequently resulted in a quickening of the pace as one or other of the pros observed, "Get a f**king move on, the boss is at the window!"

The second week of training mercifully diverged from the whole-club-forced-marching approach to a more varied regime albeit still without any ball work. The emphasis was naturally still targeted at a strict fitness regime to ensure optimum levels of stamina and conditioning in readiness for the start of the season. Training was done in squads now, with each coach taking charge of their own groups. The marching was replaced by jogging and extended runs of various distances lapping the Bellefield training grounds countless times in a stamina building aerobic programme .

As the days and weeks progressed, the pace and power of the running was increased gradually until we were doing a mix of sprint shuttle runs, hurdles circuits and agility runs through and round obstacles to improve balance and acceleration. All players had callisthenics and weight training built into the training timetable to encourage muscle development and power to improve our power to weight ratio.

Everthing that we did was done in a competitive environment. We were pitted against each other in every aspect of training whether it was a cross-country run, a sprint session, an agility exercise or weight repetitions – everything was measured, timed and recorded, including a weekly ritual every Monday morning, when every player at the club had to report for a weigh-in so that their weight could be monitored. Clearly, Everton Football Club intended to know everything they could about each player's fitness. Players who gained weight unexpectedly were given additional sessions to ensure their weight was kept at the optimum level.

For youngsters like me who were new to the professional game, this sort of training regime was light years away from anything we had experienced as schoolboys and it came as a shock. At the end of each day the apprentices changing room was full of exhausted youths who had barely enough energy to finish cleaning boots or mopping the changing room floors before they trudged off to the bus stop to wend their weary way home. In common with most of the lads, the evenings for me usually consisted of having my tea and then collapsing into bed to allow my aching muscles time to recover ready for the next day's training.

Our hard work on the training ground was eventually rewarded by the introduction of ball work into the training programme. Joy was unconfined amongst apprentices and pros alike when we were told by Stewart Imlach to get all the training balls pumped up and brought to trainers dressing room in readiness for the morning training sessions.

It was at this stage that the approach to our training changed out of all recognition. Yes we still had really punishing daily fitness work to do involving intense stamina and power running as well as gruelling weight and agility work to do. But this was now to be supplemented in each session with intensive ball skill practices and drills finishing off with five-a-side games. It was as if the whole atmosphere at Bellefield had changed. Before the introduction of the ball work, training had been undertaken in a quiet, determined almost morose atmosphere as all the players ground out those unglamorous hard pre-season miles that were essential to reaching match fitness. Hardly like a football training ground at all – more like an army boot camp at times. Afterwards Bellefield was a hive of football activity buzzing with the sound of the coaching staff shouting instructions and players responding with enthusiastic calls. Laughter took the place of the grumbles and the thud of boot and head on ball replaced the thunder of marching football boots. As Ronny Goodlass eloquently put it in the apprentices dressing room at the end of that week, "This is f**king boss isn't it lads?"

Nobody disagreed.

But amid the euphoria of training becoming more football orientated, the club had one more delight for the players to endure in the pursuit of peak fitness. It started innocently enough when Gordon West, who was the Professional Footballers Association representative for Everton was in the apprentices dressing room one Friday afternoon delivering membership cards to us all.

"Have you heard we're all going for a day out at the seaside on Monday?" he said casually.

"Are we?" we all replied innocently.

"Yes", he continued as he reached the door, "the boss has told us he's taking us to Ainsdale beach before the start of the season. It's like a thank you for all the hard work we've put in during pre-season training."

The apprentices all agreed Ainsdale was a great place for a day out to enjoy the seemingly endless miles of flat sand with the Irish Sea lapping gently beyond the towering sand dunes. Idyllic we all thought and a nice gesture from the club too.

Sure enough, not long after Gordon West had let us in on the news about Ainsdale, Stewart Imlach confirmed our visit before dismissing us early for a well-earned weekend of rest after another gruelling week of pre-season training. Strangely, he stipulated that everyone had to bring an old pair of shoes with us to wear when we were at Ainsdale rather than trainers or pumps – something with a heel on – to do with protecting Achilles tendons. Odd, but who were we to argue?

So that weekend I dutifully searched for an old pair of shoes to wear on our day out at Ainsdale on Monday. This didn't take long as I only had three pairs to my name. I settled on a pair of 'Slade' type brown brogues with one inch soles and even thicker stack-heels. I wondered how strange they would look with my Everton training gear. I needn't have worried.

When we got to Bellefield on Monday, the coach for our 'outing' was waiting on the car park bathed in the warm summer sunshine. As the entire Everton playing staff assembled on the car park, there was an incredible amount of piss-taking going on because the array of footwear on show for the trip.

Like myself one or two of the other apprentices had gone for the 'Slade' look and we got the full gambit of abuse from the first-team including Alan Ball insisting we were contestants in a Noddy Holder lookalike contest. Similarly quite a few of the pros including Harry Bennet, Archie Styles, Frank Darcy and Andy Rankin were more aligned to the 'Teddy Boy' fashion, sporting DA hairstyles and wore curled up winkle-pickers resulting in the shout of, "F**king hell, it's Cliff Richard and the Shadows!" from Gordon West as they got on the coach. Much hilarity ensued as we set off for Ainsdale, which continued until we reached our destination, when the atmosphere became strangely subdued, at least amongst the pros.

It was as we disembarked from the coach and saw that the first-team players and reserves were being paired-up at the foot of a gigantic sand dune that it dawned on us apprentices that we weren't here for a relaxing day out. Two by two the players were set off by Wilf Dixon scrambling up the almost vertical side of the huge sand dune until they reached Tommy Casey at the summit and turned to hurtle down to the bottom in a bizarre race. We all waited in stunned silence until it was our turn.

I can only describe what followed as the most agonising training any of us had ever done. Time after time we were pushed up and down a series of mountainous sand dunes until it felt as if our calf and thigh muscles would

40

burst. With each step in the soft dry sand our feet sank up to our ankles and pushed the sand backwards making progress up to the top agonisingly slow. The sun was now beating down on us and sand stuck to our sweat soaked skin. By the end of the session, which in truth probably only lasted about an hour, I can't recall any of the apprentices not throwing up as a result of the sheer exertion involved. The same could be said for most of the pros. When the coaching staff had satisfied themselves that we were sufficiently exhausted, we were allowed a short drinks break and then mercifully treated to a mini five–a-side tournament on the flat, endless Ainsdale beach beyond the dreaded dunes.

The teams were a mix of first-team players, pros and apprentices and I was delighted to be teamed up with Brian Labone, Joe Royle, Mick Lyons and Terry Darracott. Thankfully we were allowed to change into our pumps/trainers for the football. I was obviously ecstatic to be in the same five-a-side team as Brian Labone and Joe Royle but to be honest, I was so exhausted from the sand dune training that even without my brown brogue stack heeled 'Slade' shoes, I still played like Noddy Holder!

Thankfully the day at Ainsdale signalled the end of the most intensive part of the pre-season training programme. More and more of the training sessions involved match preparation including full-scale practice matches. Everyone was looking lean and sharp. Personally, I felt fitter than I had ever been as a result of the time spent on heavy physically demanding grounds duties coupled with the intensive training and conditioning we had all benefited from. I also felt as if I had settled into my new environment, formed friendships with the other apprentices and got to know the pros, the first-team players and the coaching staff to the point where I felt part of Everton Football Club.

As the end of July approached, there was buzz around the place as the anticipation of August and the start of the 1969/70 season hung in the air. It seemed to everyone that anything was possible.

* * * *

Back in Kirkby, apart from my football, things were pretty much as they had always been. Money was tight as ever, so having some extra cash coming in from my wages was a welcome boost to the household budget. It was a strange feeling to receive my first wage packet from Everton - £7 pounds in a small brown envelope along with a thin blue wage slip detailing basic wage, bonus (for during the season), tax, etc. I still couldn't quite grasp the fact that I was actually being paid to be an Everton player and I was happy and more than just a little bit proud to hand over half of my wages to my Mum for my keep – she was even happier to receive it.

My dad was still enjoying his retirement, taking a keen interest in my training at Everton in between doing his best to support his local, the Kingfisher Public House on Bewley Drive and studying form in the Racing Post. My sisters Elsie and Jean were immersed in their family lives away from Kirkby, my brother Alan was working shifts at Fords in Halewood, while Eddie had relocated to North Wales to start work for the Forestry Commission. That left David who was happily attending Mercer Vale Adult Training Centre and my mum working before and after school as a cleaner at my old school, Brookfield.

I popped back into Brookfield to see Bob Downing, my old PE teacher a couple of times during my first month at Everton. He was always glad to see any ex pupils and was genuinely interested in how the training and life in general as an apprentice was going. On one occasion I visited at the same time as Phil Thompson, who had started his apprenticeship at Liverpool FC at about the same time. It was interesting to compare our early experiences at both clubs. Although there were some differences in the routines and training methods, the one thing we had in common was a state of almost permanent exhaustion during the pre-season build up. As Bob reminded us, "I did tell you it would be the toughest thing you'd ever done".

Both Phil and I agreed he was right!

AUGUST 1969
SEASON'S GREETINGS

I f I thought the pre-season training and build up to the 1969-70 season was hectic and demanding, once August arrived the pace of life went into another gear. We were called to a meeting for all the players with Harry Catterick and the coaching staff in the Players' Lounge at Bellefield. Here, Mr. Catterick explained that with 1970 being the Mexico World Cup year, the English Football League season had been condensed into a much earlier time-frame than normal to allow for the England Squad to leave early to become acclimatised to the heat and altitude they would have to contend with during the tournament. This meant that the opening fixtures of the season would be on 8th August and matches would be completed on 8th April – earlier than anyone could remember.

As holders of the Jules Rimet trophy from 1966, England were amongst the favourites to win in Mexico and Mr. Catterick made it clear that he expected a number of Everton players to be selected for the squad that England Manager Alf Ramsey was assembling. He pointed out that everyone at Everton, from top to bottom, had a responsibility to ensure a successful season for the club, and he demanded the highest possible standards from all concerned to ensure this was achieved.

This pep talk only served to heighten the excitement at the prospect of the season getting under way as did the photo shoot which followed it. The pros were told to report onto the side of the pitch to the rear of the complex after changing into the match strip for their annual Official Squad Photograph with Manager Harry Catterick and the coaching staff. The apprentices were instructed to carry the agility benches from the store to the same location for use in the photo shoot. We hung around waiting to clear away the benches while a seemingly endless number of photographs of the team and individual players were taken. If any of us happened to venture into the background of any of the photos, we were immediately told to 'clear off' out of the way, which served as another reminder of our place in the pecking order.

In the week leading up to the first-team's opening fixture, a series of full scale practice matches was arranged at Bellefield involving the first-team squad playing against the reserves or the younger professionals and apprentices. The games were non-competitive with no tackling allowed due to the risk of injury to key first-team players.

I was delighted on one occasion when Stewart Imlach sent me, Ronny Goodlass, Mick Buckley and Peter Scott over to make up a side for the last 20 minutes of a practice game against the first-team. I was playing centre forward and was up against Brian Labone and John Hurst at the heart of the first-team defence. The games were supposed to be non-competitive but with Harry Catterick watching, I was running round like a mad dog trying to impress and the rest of my team were doing the same. I couldn't believe how much time the first-team had on the ball and how easy they made the game look. After 20 minutes of chasing shadows (I think I touched the ball three times), my team trudged off bathed in sweat and gasping for air having lost 3-0 while the first-team strolled back to the dressing rooms without a hair out of place! It was an object lesson in how high the standards at a club like Everton were and an indication of how far players like me needed to develop before they could compete at that level.

* * * *

The first-team were scheduled to play an incredible seven league fixtures during August including three midweek matches. The season could not have got off to a better start with an opening Saturday victory away to Arsenal at Highbury, with centre half John Hurst popping up with the only goal. They followed this up with another away win 2-0 at Old Trafford resulting in some rave reviews in the press about Everton's impressive attacking style of play.

The first home fixture of the season at Goodison Park was against Crystal Palace on Saturday 16th August. If there was no game for the apprentices, we were assigned to be on duty at the first-team match to set out the kit and boots in the home dressing room and to be on hand to clear the kit to the laundry after we'd watched the match from the stands. The apprentices loved this because you felt as if you were in the thick of the first-team action. For a start, we had to come in through the Players' Entrance into the main stand on Goodison Road an hour or so before the kick-off with all the attention from the supporters that involved.

At the time Goodison Park was undergoing the latest phase of its development. The old 1909 Archibald Leach designed Main Stand was being demolished to make way for the new three tier construction which would be the biggest stand in the country with all manner of innovative features including moving escalators to the upper tier, a new boardroom and conferencing and hospitality facilities. Having established their state-of-the-art training

44

ground at Bellefield [pictured above], it was Everton's intention that their ground would continue to be one of the pre-eminent facilities in English football. During its construction, the half-built new stand was a strange sight during matches as spectators used the completed sections, which seemed to be suspended in mid-air. Throughout the season the contrast between old and new was a constant feature for spectators on the Goodison Road side of the stadium as they were split between the completed sections of the massive new structure and the stately remnants of the old stand as it was demolished bit by bit to make way for its replacement.

As kick-off time approached, we were surrounded by the first-team players as they arrived for the match and went through their pre-match routines. We listened to the instructions and tactics being reinforced with individual players by Harry Catterick and Wilf Dixon as the build-up to kick-off increased in intensity. As a young apprentice and a dyed-in-the-wool Evertonian, I could hardly contain my excitement and savoured every moment. It was the stuff of dreams.

After a routine 2-1 win against Crystal Palace, the whole process was repeated the following Tuesday as Everton entertained Manchester United in the return league fixture. A massive 53,000 crowd congregated outside Goodison. With all due respect to Crystal Palace, the visit of Manchester United, winners of the European Cup barely twelve months earlier, was a special occasion. This was underlined for us apprentices as we stood outside the away dressing room and the United team filed in. United legends like Bobby Charlton, George Best, Dennis Law, Alex Stepney, Ian Ure and Willie Morgan to name a few filed in past us.

As kick-off time approached, Wilf Dixon told me to take a net full of freshly inflated practice balls down to the away dressing room. It was with some trepidation I approached the changing room door and knocked. Not hearing a reply, I opened the door and walked straight in. I was mortified as I was met by a stunned silence as Matt Busby broke off his pre-match team-talk to his Manchester United team in mid-sentence and turned to see who had interrupted him. All eyes were on me. I managed to stutter, "I, I, I'm sorry. I've erm, just brought your kicking-in balls". The legendary United manager looked at me, nodded and said in his broad North Lanarkshire accent, "Thanks son, just leave them there and be off with you".

I couldn't get out quick enough and rushed back to tell the rest of the lads I'd just interrupted the great Matt Busby's team talk! Everton ran out comfortable 3-0 winners that night. It was their fourth win on the bounce and they were building a head of steam as the season got into full swing.

By the end of August, Everton had racked up a further two league home wins against Sheffield Wednesday and Don Revie's reigning champions Leeds United. Only a draw away to FA Cup holders Manchester City prevented a 100% record for Everton in the opening month of the season. This was achieved with midfielder Tommy Jackson deputising for Alan Ball in the first game of the season and continuing for the rest of month in place of Howard Kendall who was injured in the opening fixture.

So, at the end of a challenging month of fixtures, Everton sat proudly at the top of Division 1 having dropped just one point in seven matches, scoring 14 goals and conceding just five. They were playing with flair and a swagger that enabled Joe Royle and Alan Ball to weigh in with four and three goals respectively. Things were looking up for the Toffees.

****

Naturally enough, the press and the media were showing an increasing interest in the leaders of Division 1. Hardly a day went by without there being a TV crew or radio station encamped at Bellefield with a posse of newspaper reporters and cameramen in close proximity. Adding to the heady atmosphere surrounding the training ground were the intrepid Everton supporters who congregated outside the entrance to Bellefield sometimes waiting all day for a glimpse of the first-team players and to collect autographs whenever they could. As apprentices arriving on foot, we were very careful not to engage too much with the fans and certainly not sign an autograph on the basis that we were 'only ground-staff' and for fear of being accused by the younger pros as being 'big time' resulting in the inevitable piss-taking or, even worse, a 'court case'.

Amidst this hive of football and media activity, Harry Catterick maintained a distance from the mainstream of coaching activity. He was very rarely seen in his tracksuit out on the training pitch and when he was, it was almost exclusively with the first-team squad. However, you always got the feeling that his eyes were everywhere, noticing everything that was going on. This was often reinforced with a seemingly throw-away remark to one of the reserves or apprentices about something he had noticed them do in training. If he wanted to give the impression to us that he had his finger of the pulse of everything that was going on at the club, he certainly succeeded.

This was reinforced one day when the new apprentices were told to break off from a training session with Stewart Imlach and report to Mr. Catterick who was waiting to the left of the driveway into Bellefield opposite Dougie Rose, the head groundsman's house. He was deep in conversation with who we later discovered was Mike Charters, a reporter from the Liverpool Echo and his cameraman colleague.

We listened as Mr. Catterick gave a brief outline of each of us new apprentices – where we were from, what our positions were and what our schoolboy records were before signing for Everton. We were all taken aback about how much he knew about us all even though we'd only been at the club for a matter of weeks. We then had our photograph taken with Mr. Catterick before being dismissed back to Stewart Imlach to complete our training session after Mike Charters had asked Peter Whitwood a few questions about being the only new signing who wasn't a local lad having come up from Grays in Essex.

The next day the *Liverpool Echo* did a feature article including our photograph with Mr. Catterick titled, *'Everton's young ones settle in'*...

"Six more boys with dreams of reaching the heights of soccer stardom have stepped onto the learning end of the Everton production line of talent at Bellefield in the last few weeks... what manager Harry Catterick described to me as 'this year's crop from our nation-wide search for the best in schoolboy football'.

The Everton scouting net has stretched far and wide this year and the current intake includes two boys from Liverpool, two from Kirkby, one from Manchester and another from Grays in Essex. Three of them were England internationals last season. They are all 15 years old, have now signed apprentice professional forms and at the moment are settling down to the Bellefield system under coach Stewart Imlach, who shares with coach Tommy Casey the job of developing the youngest members of the Everton playing staff.

They are outside left Ron Goodlass, Liverpool, Lancashire and England; wing half Ian Bacon, Liverpool and Lancashire; wing half Mike Buckley, Manchester, Lancashire and England; Ray Pritchard, Kirkby, Lancashire and England; centre forward Stan Osborne, Kirkby and Lancashire; centre half Peter Whitwood, Grays and Essex.

When I met them this week, Mr. Catterick pointed out the various age groups training in the sun.

The six new boys were among the squad of 16 and 17 year olds; at the far end of the pitch were the 18 years age group, who make up the 'A' team in the main; then came the Central League players whose average age is about 20; and finally the first-team, average in the early twenties, who were training without Colin Harvey and John Morrissey both away with the Football League team for last night's match in Barnsley, and Tommy Jackson with the Northern Ireland squad.

There is tremendous schoolboy talent among the latest additions to this stage but no one will attempt to predict their future.

But I do know that that the three boy internationals – Goodlass, Pritchard and Buckley attracted immense interest among senior clubs throughout the country. The potential is there abundantly, of course, and now it is being coached and encouraged along the famous youth policy lines developed by Mr. Catterick.

The end products are players like Tommy Wright, Colin Harvey, Joe Royle and John Hurst – all established first-teamers who, only a few years ago, were like the current crop of Goodlass, Bacon and company – rather shy, eager-to-learn youngsters with the football world at their feet if they can develop their schoolboy talents to tackle the fierce demands expected of a top class professional.

I wish them well. They could not be learning their trade in a more sophisticated set-up than Bellefield; the prizes and the fame are there for the taking if they dedicate themselves to the job".

Needless to say our appearance in a photograph in the Echo and the accompanying article meant that we were immediately the subject of a huge amount of ribbing, piss-taking and leg-pulling from the other apprentices and were fair game for the rest of the pros who took great delight in pointing out our new 'celebrity' status and how 'big time' they thought we had become. For example, Brian Labone was heard to say to Ray Pritchard," Ray, if you can tear yourself away from the press for a minute, can you fetch me another towel?" This caused a ripple of amusement amongst the other first-teamers.

Another typical put down was from Steve Seargeant, one of the young pros, towards Mick Buckley, when he said, "Hey Mick, I saw your photo in the Echo last night".

"Did you?" Mick replied innocently.

"Yeah and you're just as f*****g ugly in real life! Now, here, get these frigging boots cleaned", Steve added much everyone's amusement.

This was all pretty light-hearted banter in the main and we managed to laugh it off whilst making ourselves scarce in order to escape the worst of it. The coaching staff were obviously aware of what was going on but Stewart Imlach and Tommy Casey seemed to studiously avoid intervening, presumably on the basis that it was part of the toughening-up process for schoolboys moving into such a competitive environment; and to intervene on behalf of one of the hapless apprentices might have made matters worse for them.

Nevertheless, whilst usually taking the ritual mickey taking in our stride, we were all concerned when, a couple days after the Echo article had appeared, there was a sudden bang on the apprentices dressing room door before training and Alec Clarke, a young goalkeeping pro, burst in, grabbed Peter Whitwood and man-handled him into the young pro's dressing room next door.

"Court Case!" Alec shouted as the door slammed behind him.

The stunned silence was broken by Peter Scott, one of the senior apprentices, when he said, "God help him. I don't know what he's done, but he'll get slaughtered in there".

We all wracked our brains to think of what Peter might have done. He was really quiet and kept his head down all the time. He got loads of stick from most of the apprentices because he was from 'dahn sarf' and was always having the mickey taken out his southern accent. The vast majority of us were Scousers through and through as were two thirds of the pros and poor old Peter was all too often the butt of jokes and pranks.

He was also the only one out of the apprentices who was living in digs on Merseyside, which was a long way from his home in Essex. Even Les Ormerod and Mick Buckley the ex-Manchester Boys apprentices travelled from Manchester every day.

Curiosity was beginning to get the better of us and we were about to draw lots to see who would go into the dressing room next door to find out what 'charges' Peter was facing when David Johnson, another of the young pros came into our dressing room and ordered me, Ronny, Ian, Ray and Mick to follow Peter next door.

All of the young pros sat stony-faced, arms folded staring at Peter who was stood, petrified in the middle of the room. Alec was sat on the 'judge's' chair at the front of the room.

He announced, "The accused was observed on the day in question, after an interview with Mr. Catterick, undertaking an interview of his own with a reporter from the *Liverpool Echo*. He is, therefore, accused of being 'big time' and getting above his station as an apprentice. You have been brought here as witnesses. Is this what happened?"

We looked at each other nervously, all nodded, then I plucked up the courage to add in mitigation, "But he couldn't help it. The reporter started talking to him first".

"It doesn't matter", Alec shouted. "All those who find the defendant guilty as charged, raise your hand now".

The verdict was unanimous and Peter looked even more distraught.

Placing a pair of black shorts on his head by way of a judge's black cap for sentencing, Alec solemnly proclaimed that the sentence of the court was for the defendant to receive six strokes of the large Dunlop Green Flash which was reserved for such occasions. Peter tried to flee from the dressing room but was restrained by several of the pros. We were dismissed back into the apprentice's dressing room where we could hear the loud slap of Peter's punishment being administered.

When Peter came back into our dressing room, his pale face was streaked by the tears he had fought unsuccessfully to hold back. We comforted him and told him to take no notice. The Kangaroo Court was over but every one of us was glad we hadn't been in the dock. Even allowing for the fact that initiations were an inevitable part of making your way as a kid in football – or any other job for that matter, it seemed a harsh lesson to learn and an even harder punishment to be humiliated in front of your peers. The look on everyone's face made it clear that none of us wanted to be the next one in court.

Peter was very withdrawn for the next couple of days – even quieter than normal. He seemed to get on with the hectic schedule of training as normal but there were times, especially in practice matches, when he appeared to have lost a bit of confidence, particularly when up against some of the younger pros. On reflection, it was hardly surprising.

****

It was impossible to dwell on incidents like Peter Whitwood's court case because as well as the first-team having a hectic start to their fixtures, competition for places in the reserves and 'A' and 'B' teams was also hotting up as the season got under way for the rest of us.

From a personal point of view, I felt as if I'd had a good pre-season and was as fit as I'd ever been in my life. I was bursting for the chance to test my skills and ability wearing the royal blue shirt of Everton especially when the fixtures for the 'B' Team showed the opening three fixtures for August were against Liverpool (home and away), then Manchester United at home. I'd trained really hard and did everything I could to put Stewart Imlach's instructions and coaching into practice on the training ground. However, I found myself on the touchline for the first four fixtures of the season.

It was really hard watching the other apprentices getting their first few games under their belts in the 'B' Team. To be fair, I wasn't the only one of the apprentices who had to bide his time before getting their first game. I reasoned that with over 50 full-time pros and apprentices and only 44

(L-R) Ian Turner, Terry Darracott, Tommy Hughes, Terry Owen, Billy Kenny, Alan Whittle, Steve Sargeant, Bryn Jones, David Johnson, Billy Brindle, Alec Clarke

places in the starting line-ups for the four Everton teams, there had to be some players who sat it out on the substitute's bench. Added to this was the fact that there were always a number of trialists and assorted youths who had been recommended through Everton's scouting network to be accommodated in the junior teams so that the coaching staff could run the rule over them as potential signings just as myself, Eddie Avis and Mick Quinn had been at Burnley. However, it was still hard to bear, when the 'A' and 'B' team sheets were pinned up on the noticeboard at Bellefield on the Fridays before those first few games.

As no explanation to me or any of the other lads who hadn't been selected was forthcoming from Stewart Imlach, I decided that the only thing I could do was re-double my efforts in training each week and hope that I forced my way into the reckoning for the following game.

I finally realised a personal ambition by pulling on the royal blue shirt for the first time in the 'B' Team match at Bellefield against Burnley on 23rd August 1969.

It was a culmination of so much for me. Although it was just a run-of-the-mill junior Lancashire League fixture that wouldn't even register on the radar of the average Everton supporter, it was a huge step for me and my fledgling career in the professional game. I couldn't express the pride I felt when I ran out onto the pitch and saw my dad amongst the sparse gathering of parents, club officials and the odd spectator. It was a humble start......
but it was a start.

The game seemed to fly by. I enjoyed every moment of it. The team was made up of apprentices plus three trialists. Paul McEwan, my Kirkby Boys team-mate had been signed as an additional apprentice the week before and weighed in with two goals in a comfortable 3-1 victory. Stewart Imlach seemed very pleased with the win and the mood in training the week after was buoyant amongst the youngsters after Tommy Casey's 'A' Team had also beaten Burnley 5-1. There was a good rapport on the training pitch with Stewart Imlach and Tommy Casey often changing places to get a broader view of their respective squads of youngsters.

I must have done well enough in my first game as I retained my place in the 'B' team for the home match against Preston North End the following Saturday. The trialists from the Burnley game were replaced by Mick Buckley and Ronny Goodlass who had both played for the 'A' Team the previous week. Terry Darracott, one of the pros, also played after being out for some weeks with an injury. Again we ran out easy 4-1 winners, and again I felt as if I had acquitted myself well enough.

At the end of August, things were finally beginning to drop into place for me on the playing side. I felt fit, sharp and didn't feel out of place or out of my depth playing in the 'B' Team alongside the older apprentices. Some of them, including John Smith, Joe Moran and Alan Wilson had made the next step up to the 'A' Team on a regular basis and Peter Scott had broken through into Arthur Proudler's Reserves. And that was where I wanted to be playing as soon as I could. I couldn't wait for September's matches.

* * * *

If I thought life as a new apprentice professional footballer was challenging, I had a daily reminder at home of what the meaning of hard work was, in the form of my mum.

Her life was a particularly hard and demanding one. Apart from being David's full-time carer and working as a school cleaner, she had the house to clean and all the meals to organise for a hungry family. That was easier said than done in Kirkby in those days.

Thanks to the predictable lack of foresight on the part of the Town Planners, basic amenities such as shops, libraries and community centres were overlooked in their haste to clear us out from Everton and other areas in Liverpool designated for 'slum clearance'.

Consequently for many years 'shopping' in our part of Kirkby consisted of buying basic supplies and provisions from two 'vans', which has been converted into mobile shops from an old charabanc and furniture removals lorry respectively.

The 'vans' were like Aladdin's Cave inside with tightly packed shelves full of every conceivable consumable you could imagine – and all at higher prices than you could imagine! These entrepreneurs had quickly realized that

Kirkby folk had very little option but to use their facilities for shopping. The only alternative in Southdene before the Town Centre Shopping Precinct and Broad Lane shops were built, was a long bus journey into Liverpool with all the kids in tow – not really practical for the young Kirkby mums.

Frank Ainsworth, the owner of the converted furniture lorry did, to be fair, allow 'credit', which my mum had to use on a regular basis as the family budget stretched to breaking point most weeks. Frank was a thin stooping man of indeterminate age with a wrinkled, kindly face and the most bowed legs I can remember seeing. He seemed able to sense if anybody was about to ask for 'credit'. When we were younger, he often put the goods on the counter and spare any embarrassment by saying:

"Tell your mum it was three shillings and tuppence and she can pay me next week if she hasn't got the right money".

Not 'having the right money' we all knew, meant skint. We very often 'didn't have the right money' and Frank's 'credit' provided a welcome respite for my mum as she constantly struggled to make ends meet.

Frank was also an Evertonian. It might just have been my view of the world then, but everyone seemed to be an Evertonian. As kids, when his 'van' was quiet, we used to stand for hours talking to Frank about Everton. He used to tell us about the games he had seen with Dixie Dean and Tommy Lawton and their goal-scoring feats. We in turn would tell him of our heroes including Alex Young, Roy Vernon, Brian Harris and Alex 'Chico' Scott.

Dogs were also a regular part of growing up in Kirkby – every family seemed to have at least one. Our particular pooch was Lassie, a stray that my dad had found as a tiny pup in the snow on the way home from work one winter's night. Lassie (we called him Lassie even though he was male) was, as my dad used to pronounce when we asked him what sort of dog he was, a 'genuine pedigree mongrel'. This was a fact we repeated earnestly to our impressed mates who in turn told their amused parents.

Lassie was about the size of a Labrador and was predominantly black with brown legs, white paws and a white tip to his tail. He also had a great capacity for learning new tricks, which we taught him for hours on end. Begging, fetching, chasing cats, standing on his back legs and dancing, you name it and he could do it. He could sing as well. Whenever we sang Everton songs he would join in howling and yelping until my mum told us to shut up our row!

The other strange thing was that he hated Liverpool and anything red. It must have been something to do with living in a house full of Evertonians. We tested our theory by throwing my dad's old slippers for him. The blue ones he ran after and brought back placing them gently on the floor and barking excitedly for them to be thrown again. The red ones on the other hand, he used tear to shreds for no apparent reason other than them being red.

Whenever he heard that 'Liverpool song', he used to snarl, growl and bare his teeth at whoever sang it. He even tore the backside out of the milkman's trousers once because he was wearing a red scarf!

Lassie's party piece, however, was to run over to Frank's van when my mum was shopping there and carry his tin of dog food home in his mouth, ready to be fed. All anybody had to do was mention the word 'meat' and he would become feverishly excited and then shoot out of the door and across the road to the van and jump up and down at the counter until a tin of dog food was deposited in his mouth for him to take home.

The only trouble was that if he heard the word 'meat' in the wrong context, it would have the same effect. For example, one day my dad asked my mum to get some meat paste for his sandwiches for work the next day. The dog heard the word 'meat', misunderstood and ran over to Frank's van only to be dragged away crest-fallen and disappointed.

One Sunday I was at home with my brother Alan and as usual we were making our own entertainment playing with Lassie when our mum arrived home from the launderette or 'bag-wash' as it was known. Even though we had both left school and were working, we were still expected to help out with chores at home. She emptied a black bin liner full of clean clothes onto the settee and told us to make ourselves useful by folding the clothes ready for ironing. It was very boring work and we soon craved something more interesting to do. So for a laugh, we decided to dress the dog up in my dad's underpants and vest.

We put the underpants on Lassie back to front so that his tail came through the fly-hole. We then placed the vest over his head, threading his front legs through the arm holes and tucking the rest of the vest into his underpants. To finish, as we knew Lassie was an Evertonian, we decided to tie my dad's Everton scarf cravat-like around his neck. Very smart indeed we thought admiring him as he stood proudly in his new outfit, tail wagging enthusiastically through the fly-hole of the underpants.

Mum came in from the kitchen with her shopping bag and in a rush as usual and seeing Lassie modelling my dad's blue and white scarf and undies said,

"What do you think you're doing? Take those things off the dog, it looks soft! I'm off to the van".

With that she rushed out of the house heading for Frank's and leaving the front door ajar. We of course ignored what we had been told and left Lassie in his new 'outfit' and started talking about the prospect of a game of football that evening.

I said, "Ay Alan, do you fancy a game of footy with the lads tonight?"

Alan replied, "Okay. What time do they want to meet?"

That was it. At the sound of the word 'meet', Lassie's ears pricked up, he translated 'meet' into 'meat' and having seen my mum go out moments earlier with her shopping bag, he was off like a shot out of the front door, still dressed in my dad's underpants and vest with matching Everton scarf!

As he scampered off, Everton scarf blowing in the wind, across the road towards my mum at the van, we shouted him to come back, but to no avail – he was a dog on a mission. We watched helplessly as he arrived at the van where my mum was waiting to be served as he jumped up and down at the counter waiting for his tin of meat.

Seeing the dog, Frank said to my mum, "Mrs. Osborne, is that your dog? Has he been in an accident or something? I didn't know he was an Evertonian".

Looking down at the mummified mutt, my mum replied, "Take no notice, it's our Alan and Stanley messing about. You'd better give me a tin of dog meat for him".

She placed the tin into Lassie's mouth and he scooted off in the direction of home.

However, because he had been jumping up and down at the counter while he was waiting for his tin of meat, Lassie's vest had become un-tucked from his underpants and as he crossed the road in front of the house, his back legs got stuck inside the trailing vest. He was stuck fast, not able to move backward or forward.

By this time, seeing all this unfold from the front door, Alan and myself were incoherent with laughter.

Just then a green Austin 1100 came hurtling round the corner and the startled driver was faced with a dog dressed untidily in men's underwear, wearing an Everton scarf and with a tin of dog food in it's mouth and stranded in the middle of the road. He managed to apply the brakes just in time and came to screeching halt a matter of inches from the floundering animal. He got out of his car and was laughing so much that the tears were running down his face. He then lifted Lassie onto the pavement, tucked the vest into his underpants, straightened his scarf and watched open mouthed as the dog disappeared into our house. Shaking his head, the man got back into his car and drove off obviously not believing what he had just seen.

I sometimes wonder what that bloke must have thought and what he said to his wife when he got home that day. She would never have believed him about a dog dressed in men's underwear. On the other hand, an Evertonian dog in Southdene in those days – very possible.

SEPTEMBER 1969 BOOT CAMP

The momentum which Everton had built up in the opening month of the season meant that hopes were high around the club that they would maintain their form over another busy month in September. Again another seven fixtures awaited them provided they could overcome a routine second round League Cup tie away to Darlington. A single goal from Alan Ball on 3rd September saw Everton through to a third round tie later in the month away to Arsenal.

On the Saturday after the Darlington cup-tie, Everton lost their first league match of the season against high-flying Derby County at their Baseball Ground stronghold. This defeat resulted in the loss of top spot in the league but far from this heralding a dip in form for the Toffees, they powered back to the top of the table racking up four successive league wins at home against West Ham, then back to back wins away to Newcastle United and Ipswich Town and rounding off the month with a 4-2 victory at home to Southampton inspired by a Joe Royle hat trick. A goalless away draw at Highbury in the League Cup meant a replay at Goodison Park would be Everton's first fixture in October.

Joe Royle was on fire and it seemed he could do no wrong. His nine goals in the opening twelve league fixtures meant he was amongst the leading goal scorers in the country. Alan Ball was proving to be the driving force in midfield and he, along with Colin Harvey and Howard Kendall, playing the kind of 'School of Science' football synonymous with the famous Everton traditions I had been used to seeing following Harry Catterick's teams from the terraces at Goodison Park as a youngster.

Inevitably, with it being the 1970 World Cup season, prominent Everton Players began to be linked with possible call-ups to Alf Ramsay's England squad for Mexico, which was due to be finalised in the spring. Alan Ball was seen as an automatic choice in view of the fact that he was an integral part of the World Cup winning England team from 1966. His midfield partners in Everton's 'Holy Trinity', Colin Harvey and Howard Kendall were mentioned in the press as potential England internationals, as well as captain Brian

Labone, right back Tommy Wright and goalkeeper Gordon West. It was a pleasure being part of the set-up at Bellefield. The optimism that surrounded the first-team filtered through to the reserves and on down into the junior ranks. The buzz and the banter was there every day meaning everyone associated with the club was in a positive frame of mind.

Whilst the majority of training and coaching was still done in squads, there were occasions when the apprentices were involved in drills and practices for the first-team squad. For example, Wilf Dixon, the first-team coach, would ask for some of us kids to send crosses into the penalty area where he had set up a practice for Joe Royle's heading, demanding we deliver each ball accurately to the near or far post as instructed. It was quite exacting and anybody failing to perform satisfactorily was soon dispatched back to Stewart Imlach or Tommy Casey to continue their sessions with the 'A' and 'B' Teams.

Similarly, if requested, we would provide a barrage of shots from various positions in and around the penalty area to test the reactions and agility of Gordon West and reserve team goalie, Andy Rankin. This was often after they had just finished a full fitness training session with the rest of the first-team and reserve squads. As youngsters we thoroughly enjoyed these shooting sessions but the poor goalkeepers were exhausted at the end. We also considered it an opportunity to impress Wilf Dixon and the first-teamers with our skills – no harm done, we thought, in the first-team coach seeing what you were capable of.

This close up involvement with the first-team only heightened the anticipation of each match. Face-to-face with the players you got a real impression of their quality amidst a growing feeling that this might turn out to a special season for the club.

****

My third game for the 'B' Team was my first away game for Everton. We travelled along the East Lancs road to Manchester City's training ground and although we fielded a fairly strong team including seven apprentices, we were just edged out 2-1 by a more experienced and mature City side, which included a couple of full-time pros who, presumably, were getting some match practice after returning from injury.

Stewart Imlach wasn't best pleased at seeing his team lose only their second match in eight games. He had a rant at us in the dressing room afterwards, insisting that we had been 'too nice' and had not been physically aggressive enough. The coach journey back to Merseyside was a very quiet one. I don't know whether it was a reaction to our defeat, but training the following week was different than normal. Maybe we were being punished by Stewart, but our running and fitness sessions seemed to be much longer than normal resulting in far less ball work and match or five-a-side practice. Everything was ultra-competitive, even more so than normal, probably trying to instil a little more steel into our preparation in view of being 'too nice' against Man City. This was all well and good but was to have serious consequences for me.

It was Friday afternoon and I was looking forward to playing for the 'B' Team at home against Blackpool the next day. We had more or less finished the ball-skills session and were rounding it off with some stretching and warm-down exercises when, for some inexplicable reason, Stewart lined us up on the touchline of one of the pitches and we did a series of competitive sprint races across the pitch with the last player in each race having to do 20 press-ups as punishment. He then instructed us to choose a partner for piggyback races across the pitch.

Then, unbelievably, he repeated the pick-a-back races stating that you could do anything you wanted to prevent runners in front of you from winning. I was carrying my Kirkby mate Ray Pritchard and a free-for-all broke out during the race with pushing, pulling, tripping and any other foul play imaginable taking place with the inevitable spills and falls amongst the runners and riders. As we overtook them, I was tripped from behind by Joe Moran who was carrying John Smith. I landed face first in a crumpled heap on the pitch with Ray landing on top of me. As I was getting up to resume the race, my left leg was stretched out behind me as I pushed on my toes go get upright. At that moment a searing pain shot through my ankle and up the back of my calf to my knee as Joe and John landed with their full weight across the back of my leg.

I screamed out in pain and rolled over onto my back not daring to move or look down at my leg. Joe and John immediately called out to Stewart that I was injured and the race was halted.

Stewart ran to where I was lying and said, "Are you alright?"

I was so angry and the pain was so excruciating. I looked down at my ankle, which had already swollen to the size of a grapefruit. I screamed back at Stewart, "Alright? What do you think? Why did you have us tripping each other up? Someone was bound to get f**king injured!"

There was a stunned, embarrassed silence amongst the rest of the apprentices as a stretcher was sent for. Stewart was taken aback by my tirade but recovered his composure, telling me to keep my mouth shut and sending for Norman Borrowdale, the club physiotherapist to inspect the damage to my ankle. I couldn't help my outburst. Seeing my ankle and knowing the unnecessary cause of the injury was maddening and the frustration of knowing how hard I'd trained to finally start playing in the 'B' Team was just overwhelming.

Norman Borrowdale soon appeared from his Treatment Room base. He positioned my injured leg so that he could strap my legs together then supervised as I was gently eased onto the waiting stretcher and carried over to the main building by four of the other apprentices. Once in the Treatment Room, the painful process of removing the boot and sock from my injured leg was undertaken and an initial assessment of the injury undertaken. Mr. Borrowdale asked me how the injury occurred and told me I would need to have a precautionary X-ray. His assessment was that I had ruptured the outside ligaments of my ankle and probably damaged the Achilles tendon as well. I immediately asked him how long I was likely to be out for and he said that it was difficult to tell with that kind of injury but eight to ten weeks was not uncommon. I was gutted.

A taxi was ordered to take me to hospital for the x-ray and a phone call made to my dad to inform him about what had happened and to arrange for him to meet me there. The x-ray confirmed Mr. Borrowdale's assessment, which the doctor said he would confirm with him by phone. My leg was put in plaster up to the knee to immobilise it and I was told that would be on for a week, possibly two. My dad joined me at the hospital and I returned to Kirkby crestfallen and on crutches. I was instructed to stay at home and off my feet for a week before returning to Bellefield for another assessment of the injury.

Being injured was a new experience for me. Apart from the odd knock or bruise, I hadn't had to miss a match since I started playing in organised competitive matches at the age of ten. The inactivity was torture and having to be cooped up at home for a week was unbearable. I couldn't wait to be back at Bellefield, even if it meant being in the treatment room for hours on end. At least I'd be involved in the day to day activity and banter around the training ground – I'd still be an Everton apprentice, albeit an injured one.

The week passed very slowly but I was consoled by the fact that the other Kirkby apprentices took the trouble to ring me at home to see how I was doing and Paul McEwan even called round on his way home from training on one of the evenings, which I really appreciated. However, my morale wasn't helped when Paul told me that the 'B' Team had thrashed Blackpool 12-2 without me! It was with mixed feelings of dread and optimism that I reported back to Norman Borrowdale, Everton's physio on my first day back after my week's enforced immobilisation. Dread at the thought of having the plaster removed and the possibility that the injury was even worse than the first assessment had indicated; and optimism that it might be less serious.

After waiting for a few minutes outside the physio room, I was called in by Mr. Borrowdale who asked me a few questions about how the ankle was feeling. Then after climbing onto the treatment table, he began to cut the plaster casing from my leg revealing my still-swollen ankle and calf but with the addition of a mass of technicolour black, blue and yellow bruising from the knee down.

"That is a nasty one", he observed as he gently lifted my leg and felt around the ankle and the calf muscle whilst asking me to move the ankle as much as I was able, to gauge how much mobility I had in the joint. He asked me again to describe the incident in which the injury occurred after which he gave a rueful shrug and said, "Well, these things happen. We'll just have to get on with getting you fixed as quickly as we can".

Just then the door to the treatment room opened and Stewart Imlach walked in. Ignoring me, he said to Mr. Borrowdale, "Norman, can you let me have a pack of elastic bandages to keep in the locker ready for this Saturday's game. We ran out last Saturday and some of the lads wanted a strapping for the match".

Still holding my swollen ankle, Mr. Borrowdale replied, "Yes Stewart, I'll get some sent down as soon as I've finished with young Osborne's ankle".

"Right", Stewart said, turned on his heel and left the treatment room without so much as an acknowledgement that I'd returned for treatment after my injury in his training session a week earlier. I wasn't expecting any special reception, but I thought that, as I was one of his players, he might have enquired about how the ankle was.

I didn't comment at all but listened to Mr. Borrowdale explain in detail what the nature of my injury was and how it would be treated and the routine I would have to go through, receiving treatment and physiotherapy seven days a week in order to get back to fitness and playing again in the shortest time possible. Throughout the explanation, my mind kept flashing back to my outburst to Stewart as I lay injured and his reaction towards me in the treatment room moments earlier. Maybe I'd been out of order in my retort towards him, but I couldn't afford to worry about that, I was too focussed on getting over the injury and back to training and playing.

My ankle was heavily strapped up to the knee and I was told to continue on crutches for another week before graduating onto a walking stick. Over the next six weeks I underwent a strict routine every day, which comprised of completing my normal apprentice duties such as preparing kit and boots before receiving treatment while the rest of the players completed their morning training session. Treatment resumed after the lunch break during the afternoon training session and the day ended with the completion of the rest of the apprentice duties, mopping floors, showers and toilets, etc. Treatment also took place on Saturday's provided Mr. Borrowdale wasn't required to attend first-team matches. All injured players were also required to attend for treatment at Bellefield on Sundays.

Specifically, my treatment involved immersing my injured leg in very hot water for half an hour or so – water so hot that the skin on my leg up to the knee was so red it looked as if I was wearing a red sock. The idea was to get the blood flow around the injury to speed up the healing process and allow the movement of joint to be gradually restored. Once Mr. Borrowdale was happy that the injury was 'warmed up' he would introduce ultra sound and heat treatment using a plethora of space-age looking equipment which adorned the impressive treatment room at Bellefield. The treatment sessions were rounded off with a massage of the injury and manipulation to aid the repair of the ruptured ligaments in my ankle and my Achilles tendon.

Over time, due to the daily contact with Mr. Borrowdale, I built up quite a rapport with him. I was really keen to find out about the methods of treatment he was using and he was happy to give 'chapter and verse' on each piece of new equipment he used and the benefits they would provide. He was a tall, distinguished gentleman in his 50's. A straight talking Lancastrian who held no truck with any of the players, he struck an authoritative figure invariably dressed in his white doctor's coat for treatment sessions.

For example, any first-team players who were late for treatment were told to, "Bugger off to the back of the queue", when they tried to persuade him to treat them ahead of any of the apprentices or younger pros. I observed him during treatment sessions and was always impressed by the way he took the trouble to explain what he was doing and why. He was careful to map out what players could do to help themselves in-between treatments.

He was also very good at morale boosting chats to players who were, unsurprisingly, disgruntled – even depressed when their injuries weren't progressing according to plan. I was sure, even as a youngster, that the psychology he used was often as effective as the physical treatment he employed in getting players back on the pitch. This was certainly true in my case as I followed his instructions to the letter and felt the benefit as week by week I progressed from crutches, to a walking stick, then walking and eventually to slow jogging. It was a fantastic feeling to get back outside, in and amongst the rest of the playing staff as they trained at full pace, while I gradually stepped up the scale of my training and recovery one step at a time on the margins of the Bellefield training complex.

The hardest part about being injured, however, wasn't the pain or the treatment. It was far harder being in the apprentices changing room every Monday morning listening to how they had performed for the 'B' Team, the 'A' Team or even the Reserves. There was a genuine excitement as results were discussed and goals described. This developed as the week progressed towards the anticipation of the next fixture on the following Saturday. I could see how much fitter the lads were getting as each week passed and each game was played. It was difficult not to feel as if I was in limbo and being left behind as players of my age like Ronny Goodlass, Mick Buckley and Ray Pritchard began to break their way into Tommy Casey's 'A' Team having been promoted from the 'B' Team following discussions with Stewart Imlach. These discussions were not always amicable, however. It often became quite heated amongst the coaching staff when, due to injury or suspension, players from the Reserves were drafted into the first-team squad resulting in 'A' Team players being required to fill the gaps in the Reserves with the knock on effect of the 'B' Team losing their best players to Tommy Casey's side.

As the junior coach at the club, Stewart invariably lost out in any argument about selection and if his team subsequently performed badly that obviously reflected on him as coach, which ultimately had implications for his prospects at the club. Clearly, competition amongst the coaching staff was as fierce as it was amongst the players.

Because of my injury I had very little to do with Stewart in footballing terms. I was, however singled out for an increasing number of boot cleaning and maintenance jobs and other menial tasks after treatment when the others were training. Cleaning the boots was a job the apprentices hated. Rather than use polish or dubbin, we had to use Neatsfoot Oil which was a foul smelling yellow oil made from the rendered bones of cattle. It was supposed to keep the boot leather supple but I used it so frequently, the skin on my hands started to turn yellow! I became a bit an expert at re-studding boots or fitting new screw inserts into them. I even had the job of organising for training boots to be repaired at the old cobblers shop that used to be opposite Goodison Park on Walton Lane next to the Stanley Pub. All well and good but I wanted to be footballer, not a cobbler.

I was becoming increasingly frustrated at being used as a 'dogsbody' by Stewart and having discussed it with my dad, I decided that I had nothing to lose by speaking to him about it. I was in the boot room one morning when Stewart came in and I asked him straight out, "Stewart, am I going to be the only one who gets all the boots to clean. I'm sometimes here for an hour or more when the rest of the lads have gone home. Is there any chance of some help?".

"Listen son", he replied, "when you're not injured and you're training every day you'll be treated the same as everyone else. I decide what the apprentices do, so if I was you I'd concentrate on getting fit and back out on the pitch".

Whilst it wasn't the sympathetic ear I would have liked, Stewarts response made me even more determined to get fit as quickly as I could and prove to him that I wasn't just a skivvy - which I hoped was probably the reaction he was looking for.

****

The only silver lining for me during a very cloudy September was that I was able to escape the monotony of the treatment table and the drudgery of the boot room on Mondays at Childwall Hall County College.

Everton had honoured their part of the Apprentices' contacts by providing 'alternative education and training opportunities' for their youngsters. While the rest of the lads chose to attend a training centre for car mechanics every Monday, myself and Peter Scott made our way to the leafy south Liverpool suburb of Childwall and its Further Education College to pursue studies for our 'O' Level Exams. I had hobbled along on my crutches and registered for Maths, History and English Literature courses.

Being injured brought home the importance of apprentices continuing with their studies or training and reminded me of the wise words of advice given to me by Mr. Bury the Headteacher of Brookfield before I left school to join Everton.

Hidden away along a tree-lined drive, Childwall Hall County College was an angular, modern fifties-designed building erected on the site of the ancient Childwall Hall. It attracted a wide range of students including trainees from the Post Office, Fire Service Cadets and Police Cadets, many of whom were attractive young ladies immaculately turned out in their Police Cadet uniforms whenever they were in college, which Peter and I were pleased to note was also on Mondays.

The atmosphere was very relaxed. The teachers and lecturers were very informal and made it clear that we were responsible to our employers if we didn't attend or fell behind with our studies and that they wouldn't be chasing after us if course work and exam preparation wasn't completed. It was much as I would have imagined it would be like as a student at university or a Higher Education College.

The quality of the teaching was good with most students being self-motivated and engaging readily with the staff resulting in attendance levels at lessons invariably being high. The facilities were modern and inviting especially the college refectory, which was the social hub of the campus. This was where the students spent a lot of time mixing and getting to know each other. Inevitably questions were asked about where we worked as many of the students, like myself and Peter, were on day-release from their employers to improve their qualifications. The fact that Peter and I were apprentices at Everton caused a certain amount of interest amongst some of our fellow students, particularly the ones who were Evertonians. Sadly, the attractive female Police Cadets had no interest in football and, therefore, showed little interest in us. However, this didn't stop us from engaging them in what we thought was witty conversation every time they happened to be in the refectory at the same time as us. Needless to say, they remained singularly unimpressed, but we did get to know two of them – a stunning blonde called Mandy and an equally attractive brunette named Debbie – a little better as they shared our Maths group on Monday mornings.

So for me, a month that started so disastrously, ended up with me nursing my injury towards a gradual recovery and looking forward to October and the possibility of regaining full fitness if things went according to Mr. Borrowdale's plans for me.

OCTOBER 1969
UNION DUES

The opening game of October saw Everton entertain Arsenal in the 3rd round League Cup replay at Goodison Park. A single goal from Howard Kendall saw the Toffees through to the 4th round where they were drawn away to Manchester City later in the month.

It was back to business as usual in the league with a 3-2 away win at Wolves and a 3-1 victory at home against Sunderland. Sandwiched in-between these two wins for Harry Catterick's high-fliers, they surprisingly dropped a point away to a struggling Crystal Palace but were still in pole position in the Division 1 when they travelled to Maine Road for their mid-week League Cup-tie against Manchester City.

There was a bit of a stir around Bellefield when news broke that Catterick was going to rest a number of the first-teamers. Typically, it was groundsman Sid McGuinness who casually announced the news to us when he popped into the dressing rooms as he often did for a gossip. Always in the know, Sid said that he'd heard the boss discussing the team for the cup-tie with first-team coach Wilf Dixon and reserves coach Arthur Proudler. As usual, Sid's inside knowledge proved to be spot-on when the team was announced. Colin Harvey and Alan Ball were replaced in midfield by Tommy Jackson and debutant youngster, Billy Brindle. Up and coming central defender Harry Bennet took the place of John Hurst at the heart of the defence, with Alan Whittle and Gerry Humphries starting in the forward line in place of Jimmy Husband and Johnny Morrissey.

Needless to say Billy Brindle, as a local lad making his first-team debut, got loads of stick from the other reserves about being 'big time' having made it to the first-team squad for the first time. Sadly, it was to be a disappointing debut for Billy as Manchester City ran out 2-0 winners and went on to beat West Bromwich Albion in the final at Wembley in the spring of 1970.

One player who didn't get a chance in the first-team was third string goalkeeper Geoff Barnett who seldom got the nod during his seven years at Everton. It happened so quickly that not even Sid McGuinness could foresee his transfer to Arsenal for £35,000 as an emergency replacement for Bob

The PFA rule book with cup run payment details

Wilson who had broken his arm. As understudy to both Gordon West and Andy Rankin with opportunities in the first-team extremely rare, it was a move he simply couldn't turn down.

Normal service and team selection was restored for the remaining two league fixtures in October with a thumping 6-2 demolition of Stoke City at Goodison followed by a 1-0 win away at Coventry City to consolidate Everton's position as league leaders and the team in top form, closely followed by Leeds United, who had been the Bookies' pre-season favourites to win the title.

Joe Royle continued to add to his goals tally with another five in October, with Johnny Morrissey weighing in with three. Joe had been nominated as club penalty-taker for the season and had scored three during October's matches taking his total to five penalties for the season so far. His penalty taking style was unique – nothing subtle about it. He would take a run up from outside the penalty area and simply lash the ball as hard as he could straight down the middle of the goal. Joe was a big man and the sight of him bearing down on the spot kick must have been terrifying for the goalkeepers. So much so, it was difficult to get any of the keepers at Everton to go in goal when he was practicing his penalties at the end of training sessions.

Back at Bellefield, the general feeling was that the omission of five first-team players against Manchester City for the League Cup tie underlined where Harry Catterick and the Everton board saw their priorities for the season and how serious the pursuit of the club's first Division 1 title for six years was being taken.

****

All the players at the club were fully signed up members of the Professional Footballers' Association and Everton could not have had a more popular PFA Representative than Gordon West. He was actually the first one of the first-team squad to introduce himself formally to the new apprentices after we'd started. He burst into the apprentices' dressing room unannounced one morning and bellowed in his clipped Barnsley accent, "Right you little bastards, get your hands off your cocks and listen up!"

There was a moment's startled silence, then the room full of adolescent apprentices burst into hysterical laughter as we saw Gordon West, the first-team goalkeeper, dressed in a full tracksuit with huge pair of underpants pulled on over the top and hoisted up to his chest – hilarious! He then retorted, "What are you f**king laughing at? I'm here on serious business! I'm your PFA Rep!" It certainly grabbed our attention!

Gordon was a regular visitor and took the trouble to explain to us all the role of the Professional Footballers' Association and how he was the elected representative for Everton Football Club. He explained in great detail the benefits of membership of the PFA – they paid exam fees for any apprentices who carried on with their academic studies or ensured alternative vocational training was offered. They were also available to represent players who had any contractual disagreement with their clubs. We quickly forgot Gordon's often comical demeanour and earnestly engaged with what he had to say – all very informative and enlightening.

That was very much Gordon West's style – wickedly funny, but at the same time deadly serious and intense. He regularly added to the atmosphere around Bellefield with his humorous interludes. For example, he once strode into our dressing room dressed only in a jock strap, strumming 'air guitar' and singing at the top of his voice (to the tune of 'Oh Boy' by Buddy Holly),

"All of my life, I've been kissin', your left tit, 'cos the right one's missin', Oh Boy!"

And I don't know whether he coined the lyric, but on another occasion, again strumming 'air guitar', he regaled the first-team dressing room with (to the tune of 'You can't do that' by the Beatles),

"I've got something that might cause you pain, It's nine foot chopper with a varicose vein!"

Both of these musical anecdotes from Gordon had the assembled audiences in stitches and were typical of the knock about humour and buoyant mood at the club as morale soared and Everton topped the league and looked an increasingly good bet for the Championship.

But there was another side to Gordon West though, which began to emerge as I observed him at close quarters as the season unfolded.

Firstly, there were difficulties , which Gordon had to overcome related to his physique and temperament. He was a big, stocky man and as such had difficulty keeping his weight under control – this had nothing to do with his diet or attitude to training – he just had a tendency to keep weight on. In fact I would say that he trained harder than anyone else at the club and went to extraordinary lengths to lose excess pounds. I remember at one stage, in an attempt to 'sweat down', his kit for training consisted of his normal kit, a thick Aran jumper followed by a full length plastic mac, with another tracksuit on top! There were occasional terse comments and conversations between Gordon and Harry Catterick or Wilf Dixon about his weight, which they insisted on checking virtually every day.

With regard to Gordon West's temperament, it was a shock to me as a young apprentice and long-standing Evertonian and fan of his to see the contrast between his confident, humorous persona in training or between the posts on match days and the nerve-wracked character we saw during the pre-match build up to Everton first-team matches if we were on duty in the home dressing room at Goodison Park. He was literally a nervous wreck, pacing up and down, hands shaking, muttering oaths under his breath and very often being physically sick before he went out onto the pitch. However, in spite of his weight problems and his nervous disposition, Gordon was Harry Catterick's automatic choice as first-team 'keeper.

On a personal note, Gordon ensured that myself and Peter Scott received any communication from the PFA that related to education and training. One circular from Mr. R. N. Kelly, the Education Officer of the PFA was sent from their Manchester office and summarised their support for apprentices:

"Dear Mr. Osborne,

One of the services offered by the Professional Footballers' Association is advice, guidance and even financial assistance for Further Education.

The need for this is obvious. A career as a Professional Footballer can be most rewarding but it is usually fairly short. A small percentage of Players continue in the game as Managers, etc. but the majority must prepare themselves to take up employment in other fields after retirement.

It is never too early to think about this. Far too often Apprentice Professionals have given up their Further Education Courses and far too many Players are being faced with choosing a second career without any training or qualifications.

Because of this, Clause 5 of your agreement with your Club ensures that '…..the Club shall, at the request of the player or his parent or guardian, allow the Player to continue his Further Education or take up suitable Vocational Training.'

The Management of your Club will be willing to discuss the matter with you, a few clubs even have their own Education Officers, and advice is avail-

able from the PFA Education Department. Do not hesitate to contact me at the above address. If you are in any doubt, have a word with your Club's PFA Delegate who is Mr. G. West.

Yours sincerely, R. N. Kelly, Education Officer"

* * * *

Apart from correspondence, Gordon also ensured that all players at the club were supplied with the latest copy of the Rules of the PFA and a booklet called 'Extract from the Regulations of The Football League Ltd – For the information of Professional Players, Season 1969/70'. Most of these invariably found their way into the bins after being casually discarded by the players who were more interested in training and finding out which Everton team they had been selected for on Saturday.

Being injured and having time on my hands between treatment sessions, I was able to read the booklets in detail and learned some intriguing facts about the workings of the PFA and the regulations governing the organisation and management of The Football League. For example, the Management Committee of the PFA at the time consisted of the following luminaries of the game:- Terry Neill (Arsenal F.C. – Chairman), Bobby Charlton (Man Utd), Derek Dougan (Wolves), D.W. Gibson (Leicester City), A. Leighton (Bradford City), N. Lawton (Brighton and Hove Albion), Maurice Setters (Coventry City) and Terry Venables (Spurs). The PFA Booklet explained all of the functions and terms of reference of the association including Conditions of Membership, Benevolent and Insurance Funds as well as Hardship and Death Grants. Clearly, since it's foundation in 1907, the PFA had developed many facilities in support of footballers.

Even more interesting was the Extract of Regulations from the Football League. Through reading this information, it was possible to get a view of what the wage structure was like in the professional game at the time. Whilst it didn't give explicit information about the private detail of individual players' contracts, it laid out the minimum wage levels for different players within the game. Some of the more interesting facts I deduced were:-

Everton paid the apprentices the maximum allowed ie. £7, £8 & £10 per week according to their age when the minimum was a £5 flat rate.

Full-Time Players aged 20 or over had a minimum wage of £780 per annum in Division 1, £728 pa in Division 2, £676 pa in Division 3 and £624 pa in Division 4. Clubs were to pay a minimum match bonus in League and League Cup matches of £4 for a win; £2 for a draw.

Minimum bonuses for winning in each round In the FA Cup ranged from £4 in Round 1 up to £20 and £25 in the semi-final and final respectively.

Minimum bonuses for the FA Youth Cup started at £1 in Qualifying Rounds and Round 1 to £6 for winning the final.

Where whole matches were televised (not including highlights), each player taking part was paid £10.10 shillings from the fee the club received from the television company.

These wages even for young full-time professionals were obviously not astronomic. As a comparison, I worked out that my brother Alan, who was working at Fords Halewood production line earned a basic of around £20 per week plus shift allowances meaning he received an annual wage of just over £1000 per annum.

Obviously it was impossible to know what the first-team players were earning because they all had clauses in their contracts, which supplemented their basic wage with bonuses for results and other performance related factors. We often caught the drift of conversations in the first-team dressing room relating to bonus payments for such things as League Position, League points totals, goals scored and even crowd attendances at Goodison for home games. Whatever the individual circumstances, the mood was always upbeat when discussing wages due to the fact that Everton were riding high in the league with the associated financial rewards being reaped by the players. That being the case, Gordon West had no problems collecting the PFA Union dues when they were required.

* * * *

From my own point of view, receiving this information from the PFA provided a small measure of reassurance at a time when my morale was very low. Norman Borrowdale insisted that my treatment was progressing as expected but I was still impatient to be back out training with the other apprentices instead of in the treatment room or cleaning stacks of dirty boots when Stewart Imlach felt the need.

Throughout September and October, the treatment I had been receiving meant that I was able to step up the training I was doing under Mr. Borrowdale's supervision. Gradually I was able to increase the amount of running I was doing, progressing from jogging to sprinting then introducing twisting and turning and finally moving onto ball work. I was allowed to join Stewart and the rest of the apprentices for some sessions and eventually, Mr. Borrowdale signed me off to train as normal with permission to take full part in all aspects of training.

This was a huge relief to me and I relished the chance to get back into the full swing the normal routine with the rest of the Everton youngsters – and get away from the smell of dirty boots and Neatsfoot oil at last!

I knew I had an awful lot of work to do to get back up to the fitness level I was at before my injury and catch up with the rest of the apprentices. Some the other lads had had injuries as well during my lay-off but they were mainly knocks and muscle strains, which they were quick to recover from given one or two weeks treatment. It was approaching seven weeks since I last played in the 'B' Team and I knew competition for places was even more fierce than before. During my absence Stewart's team had played seven matches, winning three, drawing two and losing two. This mixed bag of results gave me some hope as November approached that if I did enough in training sessions with the 'B' Team squad Stewart might reward me with a recall to his side.

NOVEMBER 1969
PRIVATES ON PARADE

November's fixtures for Everton's first-team promised some respite from the congested schedule of matches they had played during the opening three months of the season when they played at total of 21 matches, seven in each month.

In their first game of November, a crowd of almost 50,000 at Goodison Park saw Everton maintain top spot in Division One with a 1-0 win over Nottingham Forest with right-back Tommy Wright scoring a rare goal for the Toffees. This was followed by an uncharacteristically below par performance away to West Bromwich Albion seeing the Baggies run out comfortable 2-0 winners.

Everton's title aspirations were dealt another blow in their next match, when they dropped a point away to Chelsea, who had been near the top of the table since the start of the season. This disappointment was compounded by the fact that Colin Harvey picked up an injury, which was to see him out of first-team action for two months.

As a key member of the Everton midfield which operated around Harvey's intricate interplay with Howard Kendall and Alan Ball, it was a huge blow for them. The final game of November saw Tommy Jackson deputise for Harvey in a 2-1 home victory over Burnley. This win was sufficient to keep Everton ahead of a group of teams including Leeds Utd, Chelsea, Wolves, Man Utd and Liverpool who were all vying with Everton to be league leaders heading into December.

Tommy Jackson was to wear the Everton number six shirt throughout Colin Harvey's injury. Having replaced injured Alan Ball and Howard Kendall in an unbeaten run of seven matches in the first month of the season, Tommy was no stranger to the first-team and was a reliable replacement. He didn't have the same flair and swagger as Kendall, Ball or Harvey but made up for this with a dogged determination, which saw off so-called higher profile opposition midfield players from other leading clubs. Supremely fit, Tommy was a handful and put his combative style of play to good use in the absence any of Everton's midfield maestros.

Off the pitch, Tommy Jackson was a quiet unassuming character. In contrast to Colin Harvey's outgoing lively persona, Tommy seemed an easy-going, almost introverted person. He spoke in a soft Ulster lilt, always asking the apprentices politely for kit or boots when he required them, rather than using the raucous demands we often encountered from some of the other pros. He also took an interest in the youngsters at the club and often encouraged or advised them if he was training in the same group or playing in a practice match with us. He was a gentleman and we were all quietly pleased when he got his run in the first-team.

        * * * *

The start of November thankfully saw me restored to full fitness. The extra work I had done with Mr. Borrowdale and the full-scale training back with Stewart and the other apprentices meant that I was ready to take my chance back in the 'B' Team when it came. Stewart must have noticed this because I was recalled to his team against Preston North End in a strong line-up that included Peter Scott, Mick Buckley, Ronny Goodlass, Ian Bacon and Davey Graham, all of whom had had several matches in either the 'A' Team or the Reserves. It was pleasure to finally be playing again and I was delighted to score two goals in a 5-0 win after being set-up twice by Ronny Goodlass's fantastic wing play on the left flank.

Even though it was a lowly 'B' Team game in the Lancashire League, I couldn't begin to describe what it was like, as an Evertonian, to actually score a goal for Everton. I'd been used to scoring goals and lots of them as a schoolboy, but to get my name on the score sheet for the first time for my club, wearing the famous blue shirt was unforgettable.

This was the first of an unbeaten run four matches for me and the 'B' Team in November including further home wins against Bury (4-0), Oldham Athletic (2-0) and an away victory at Blackpool (1-0). I also added a third goal to my total in the game against Oldham.

Maximum points in the four games and twelve goals scored without reply meant that Stewart was delighted with the results. I was playing with the confidence that four games in succession and three goals to my name naturally gave me. I felt as if I was as fit as anyone of the apprentices and made sure that I was at or near the front in any running or fitness routines we were put through to try to underline to Stewart that I was fully committed to keeping my place in his team. I hoped that overcoming the injury, regaining full fitness and playing my part in the 'B' Teams successful run of results might even change Stewart's relationship with me bearing in mind how dismissive he had been of me following my outburst on the day I was injured in his training session. If his attitude towards had changed, however, it wasn't

Action from an 'A' Team match played at Bellefield

obvious although I contented myself with the fact that he had continued to select me; I also spent a lot less time cleaning boots!

* * * *

Due to my enforced absence from training with the apprentices during most of September and October, I had been 'promoted' to being involved with the duties catering for the first-team dressing room. This was very much a double-edged blessing for me. On one hand I got to mix and rub shoulders with the likes of Kendall, Ball, Harvey, Labone, Morrissey and Royle, on the other hand, we apprentices were the butt of many a prank or initiation that was doing the rounds. I remember being sent to the physio's room to ask for a glass splint and the old favourite of the 'pull the apprentice's shorts down when he's hanging up the kit' trick, which most of us were subjected to at some stage.

Running the gauntlet in the first-team dressing room was offset, however, whenever Sid McGuinness, the assistant groundsman brightened up our afternoons in the apprentices' dressing room. As well as being well up on any rumours that were circulating around the club about prospective signings, he was a fund of jokes and funny stories, which he regaled us with whenever he dropped in. More importantly to us adolescent young men, he would let us borrow his latest collection of Girlie Mags, with all the attraction that that would obviously have. This was especially true when in the 1960's the raunchiest thing you were likely to see on TV was The Tiller Girls on Sunday Night at the London Palladium or Angela Rippon exposing her legs on the Morecambe and Wise Show. To have copies of the latest *Parade*, *Fiesta* and *Men Only* was too good to be true for the Everton Apprentices and resulted in many an unseemly rush to get hold of said magazines. Little did Sid know, however, his kindness was to result in the most embarrassing moment, if not of my life, then certainly of my brief Everton career so far.

The day started like any other. Training in the morning, light lunch followed by apprentices drying and hanging kit in the pros dressing rooms ready for the afternoon session. Apprentices were then allowed a short break before the afternoon training session began.

Sid arrived with a fresh batch of every apprentice's favourite mags, one of which I manage to secure after an initial scrummage. I then entered a world of my own in the company of Vivacious Sue from Stevenage and Gorgeous Gale from Taunton. I was just enjoying Parade's Centrefold, Delectable Diane from Dawlish when I was brought back to reality by screaming from along the corridor in the direction of the first-team dressing room.

"Stan, Stan it's Labby. You haven't put his towel out, he's going f**king mad!" It was Mick Buckley's voice. Panicking, I dropped my well-thumbed magazine to the floor and stood up. From the expressions on the faces of the other apprentices and the tent-like bulge at the front of my shorts, it was obvious that Sue, Gail and Diane had made quite an impression on me.

"You can't go in there like that!" Ray Pritchard insisted. It was too late. I could hear the shouting from the first-team dressing room getting louder and it was definitely Brian Labone's voice. The Captain of the club for God's sake!

Now getting a sixteen-year-old's erection to subside on demand is the proverbial mission impossible. So trying not to panic any more than I already was, I pulled my tracksuit top down as far as I could over my embarrassing volcanic appendage, grabbed a spare towel and ran awkwardly and half bent forward towards the awaiting irate 'Last Corinthian' in the first-team dressing room.

All went well at first as, holding the spare towel in front of me to disguise my still-stiff member, I walked into the dressing room half stooping like Quasimodo to find Brian Labone sitting changed ready for training quietly reading his daily paper, with the rest of the first-team sitting around casually chatting.

"Sorry about that Brian, we were a bit busy. I've brought your towel now. Where do you want it?" I enquired.

"Hang it on the peg", he replied, not even glancing up from his paper.

I edged self-consciously forward to where Labby was sitting and carefully reached up with the towel to hang it on his peg. Just as I was at full stretch and with my tracksuit top riding up my torso, somebody whipped my shorts down!

There was a stunned silence, all eyes were on me and in particular my tumescent adolescent penis as it hung forward, tapping rhythmically on the top edge of Brian Labone's newspaper just above a headline about the Vietnam War that read ironically, 'Yanks To Pull Out Soon'.

So there I stood, suspended in time and space, eye to Jap's eye with the legend and institution within Everton Football Club that was captain Brian Labone. Tension filled the air. Everyone waited for Brian's response. How would he react?

It was with all the unflappable composure he displayed at the heart of Catterick's Everton defence throughout his distinguished career. He glanced up momentarily at my throbbing appendage and immediately returned his gaze to his newspaper before coolly announcing,

"Stan, you're going to make some girl very happy one day!"

DECEMBER 1969
STATE OF
THE NATION

I couldn't remember a more keenly anticipated Merseyside Derby match than the one that opened Everton's fixtures for December. The Toffees deservedly sat proudly at the top of the league having lost only twice and playing with a flair and style that had them firmly established as the bookies' favourites to be crowned champions at the end of the season. Even more enjoyable for supporters and players alike, Bill Shankly's Liverpool were being left behind in the wake of a team that seemed destined to rule the roost on Merseyside for some time to come. As luck would have it, the 'B' Team had no scheduled match for 6th December and so any apprentices not selected for the 'A' Team game against Man Utd were instructed to report for kit duty to Goodison for the eagerly awaited showdown against our neighbours.

The atmosphere was electric as we pushed through the 57,000 fans who were milling around the ground when we arrived to help hang out the kit and boots in the home dressing room. There was an added air of heightened tension in the dressing room as Harry Catterick began his team talk explaining the importance of the match not only in terms of maintaining top spot in the league, but also to ensure pride of place for Everton in the city in the eyes of the fans.

We took our places in the Main Stand ready to savour every moment of what was always a thrilling spectacle. Goodison Park was rocked to its famous foundations when the teams emerged from the tunnel to the shrill strains of 'Z Cars' and reverberated as the thunderous and raucous chanting and singing of both sets of supporters echoed to the rafters and beyond.

Then disaster struck.

As an innocuous speculative Peter Thompson cross from Liverpool's left flank was floated into Everton's goal area, Sandy Brown, our left back launched himself at the ball in an attempt to head it out for a corner only to succeed in planting it into the roof of the net for what was to become one of the most infamous own goals ever scored. As the Liverpool fans celebrated riotously, the Evertonians were becalmed with the shock of what they had just witnessed, while Sandy Brown picked the ball out of Gordon West's goal wishing the ground would swallow him up. Everton never really recovered from this set-back and seemed in a state of trauma as their form deserted them with Liverpool taking full advantage to secure a deserved 3-0 win.

It was a morose and subdued home dressing room that we returned to after the match. Barely a word was spoken. None were needed, save the odd condolences to poor Sandy Brown who sat in dejected silence while his team-mates showered and then dressed around him. It was interesting to note the reaction of manager Harry Catterick and coach Wilf Dixon. No histrionic rants, no berating of Sandy Brown or the team as a whole, no reprisals. Just a calm assessment by Catterick himself before the players left culminating with, "Let today be a lesson to all of you. We're at the top of the league and that's where every team we play wants to be. We are there to be shot at. If we remember what happened today and maintain our normal standard of play, we'll be champions at the end of the season".

All the players seemed to take heart from this – except Sandy Brown who was inconsolable.

It was a great pity for him that his spectacular own goal halted Everton's run of results in such a high profile game as the Derby. Up to that point, he had been an ever-present in the team at left-back where he cut an intimidating figure for any opposing forwards. A dour, rugged and athletic Scot, he was ruthless in the tackle to the point where he was no stranger to the referee's notebook or the early bath. In training and around Bellefield he was not one to use two words when one would suffice and rarely joined in the banter which flowed constantly. Sandy liked his own company and began each training session with a bewildering solo routine of stretching and loosening exercises, which he had put together himself. Powerfully built and amazingly supple, he gave the impression that he was double-jointed with some of the positions he was able to contort himself into.

Whilst not a technically gifted player, he added much needed steel to a multi-talented Everton set-up, which Harry Catterick used by occasionally deploying him as a utility player in midfield in front of the central defenders or as an emergency striker when required. He was popular amongst the Everton faithful for his combative approach and was famous for possessing one of the most powerful shots in the game, having once had the speed of his strike measured at 70mph.

Sandy Brown's versatility did not, however, prevent Everton from seeking to improve their squad and typically, it was Sid McGuinness who alerted us to the prospective signing of England International left-back, Keith Newton from Blackburn Rovers. Sure enough, within a week of Sid breaking the news, Newton arrived at Goodison Park for a fee of £80,000 and was immediately drafted into the first-team to provide guile and accurate passing out of defensive situations as opposed to Sandy Brown's more direct and physical approach. Keith Newton became Everton's first choice left-back restricting Sandy to the substitute's bench and a handful of senior appearances until his Everton Career finished when he was transferred to Shrewsbury Town the following season.

The calm reaction after the defeat to Liverpool continued the following Monday when training resumed. There was no sign of panic or visible loss of confidence. It was business as usual with the first-team squad determined to put right the loss of vital points against their fiercest rivals. Other results had meant that, in spite of losing the Derby match, Everton remained at the top of the league. Their response was emphatic. A 1-0 away win against West Ham United was followed by single goal victories at home to Derby County and Manchester City. Evertonians remained positive in spite of two wasted journeys to London after their match with Spurs was postponed due to snow, and then later in the month, abandoned at 0-0 because of floodlight failure to be re-arranged later in the season. Even a 2-1 away loss at title challengers Leeds United wasn't enough to prevent Everton retaining their lead in the Championship at the turn of the year.

The run of fixtures in December saw the emergence of Alan Whittle in the Everton forward line in place of the injured Jimmy Husband. Instantly recognisable with his shock of blonde hair and lightening turn of speed, he scored a spectacular individual winning goal at West Ham running half the length of the pitch and also scored the winner at home against Manchester City. Another product of the Everton Youth set-up, he burst onto the scene providing further evidence of the talent being nurtured in the Reserves to bolster the senior squad as the club looked forward to the possibility of securing the league title in the second half of the season.

****

With only one fixture scheduled for the 'B' Team for December, I was determined to build on the run of matches I'd played in November following my long lay-off through injury. Blackburn Rovers provided the opposition at Bellefield and I was glad to see my name on the team sheet alongside seven other apprentices and three trialists.

We proved far too strong for the visitors and built up a 4-0 lead as the closing stages of the game approached. Ian Bacon had just secured the third goal of his hat-trick when my game was over. As I landed after challenging for an in-swinging corner, I went right over on my right ankle. From the pain and the swelling on the outside of my ankle, I knew it was a serious injury as I hobbled off and was replaced by the substitute. Again I cursed my luck as I sat with my dad in the casualty department at Walton Hospital waiting for a precautionary X-ray.

Reporting to Norman Borrowdale at Bellefield with the other players who were on the injured list the following morning was the last thing I wanted and the thought of another enforced extended absence from training was truly depressing. I felt as if another mountain had been placed in front of me after having to fight my way to the top of one during September and October.

But any thoughts of self-pity or hopes of receiving any sympathy were dispersed when Norman wagged his finger in my direction and said bluntly, "Now don't dare come in here with your arse in your hands thinking you're the only bugger who's got another injury. Four or five weeks work on that ankle and you'll be right. Now keep your head up and get on with it – or else!"

With Norman you always knew where you stood and his plain speaking was probably just what I needed. At least I had an approximated time frame for recovering from this latest set-back and I figured that with no more fixtures for Stewart Imlach's team until early January, there was a chance for me to be nearing fitness early in the New Year and not miss too many games. But this crumb of comfort was small consolation as the monotonous grind of treatment sessions began again and of course Stewart made sure I was re-acquainted to my old friend Neatsfoot Oil in the boot room!

* * * *

The tradition at Everton was that as each Christmas approached, The Chairman and Board of Directors of the club would visit Bellefield to meet the players and staff with the Chairman or eminent member of the Board delivering a 'State of the Nation' address on how the fortunes of the club were progressing and what their expectations were.

So, on Christmas Eve, it was to a packed, hushed and attentive Players' Lounge that none other than Cecil Moores, began his speech. Flanked by the great and good of the Club's hierarchy he underlined the proud traditions that had been the hallmark of the club with its guiding motto 'Nil Satis Nisi Optimum' emphasising that, indeed, only the best was good enough. He praised the Manager, Harry Catterick and his first-team squad for their efforts so far in reaching the top of the first division and stated that his expectation was that the Championship would be secured come the end of the season. He also acknowledged the development of home-grown talent through the youth set-up as a major source of new first-team players but added that the club would not hesitate to spend the necessary resources to bring in the best from other clubs, if necessary, in order to ensure Everton remained at the pinnacle of the English game. As an Evertonian, I felt an enormous sense of pride listening to his words.

Then, having wished us all the best of Christmases, he announced that a Luxury Littlewoods Christmas Food Hamper would be delivered that afternoon for each of the players and staff of the club by way of a thank you to everyone for their efforts during 1969.

So, inspired by Mr. Moores words, and eager to know what was in the Littlewoods Food Hampers, the apprentices set about distributing the large brown boxes that had been stacked at the side of the indoor training pitch by the delivery van driver. Having completed that task, Stewart and Tommy Casey wished us a brief 'Merry Christmas' before we were dismissed, heavily laden with our own hampers.

* * * *

Making my way home on two buses carrying a heavy, cumbersome hamper box was easier said than done, especially with a heavily strapped ankle. But that's what I had to do along with Ray Pritchard and Paul MacEwan – all the way back to Kirkby.

It was a pleasant surprise to my mum when she opened the front door and I staggered into the house carrying my hamper. After explaining that it was a gift from Everton F.C. we set about emptying the hamper of its contents. Having not previously had the financial wherewithal to afford a Christmas Hamper in our little corner of Kirkby, let alone a Littlewoods Luxury Christmas Hamper, the prospect of having additional food and provisions over the festive period was most welcome as we examined each item we unpacked. A veritable feast was unearthed including traditional Christmas fare such as a Christmas pudding, a Christmas cake, tins of fruit and vegetables, Brazil nuts, a bottle of wine, a bottle of sherry, a stuffing mix, cheese & crackers and butter. There were also some seldom seen exotic items like Danish tinned ham, Belgian truffles, Turkish Delight and some pretty fancy Christmas Crackers and foil wrapped dark chocolate mints. Each item was removed from the hamper to various 'Oohs and Ahhs' from my mum and stacked on the small kitchen table.

All went straight forwardly enough until we came to the final item in the hamper and we both looked curiously at a strange stubby, green, warty-skinned, half fruit, half vegetable 'thing' about the size of a tennis ball, which my mum held aloft to get a better view. Neither of us had a clue what it was but my mum said that my dad was sure to know because he'd been all over the world with the army during the war and had seen all manner of weird, wonderful and exotic things on his travels. But when he arrived home from the pub he didn't recognise what it was either, but he maintained that our Alan would know what it was because he worked at 'Denny's Fruit and Veg' for a while straight after he left school. Frustration grew when Alan couldn't identify the mystery object either and exasperated and as a last resort my dad said to my mum, "I suppose her Majesty next door will know what it is. She's always going on about how bloody posh her family are".

He was referring to Mrs. Powell, our next door neighbour who had a reputation for being a bit full of her own importance. So, desperate to solve the mystery and swallowing her pride, my Mum went around to Mrs. Powell and asked her to come round and put us out of our misery. She came immediately, obviously keen to impress us as the font of all knowledge.

My mum handed her the mysterious item and squinting through her horn-rimmed spectacles, Mrs. Powell studied it carefully for few moments, before taking a big breath and breaking the tension by announcing, "That, if I'm not mistaken, is an avocado pear!"

JANUARY 1970 PLACE YOUR BETS

By the turn of the year into 1970, the odds of Everton retaining their grip on top spot in League Division 1 and lifting the trophy as champions at the end of the season had shortened considerably but the early months of the New Year were to prove a difficult period for them.

A 2-1 away exit from the 3rd round of the FA Cup against Sheffield United belied Everton's cup pedigree in England's pre-eminent knockout competition. Disappointing though this was, as with their early exit from the League Cup, it was assumed by most commentators that priority was being given to the league campaign, whilst the cup competitions were of secondary importance to the league leaders.

The swagger returned to Everton's play in their first league match of 1970, sweeping aside Ipswich Town 3-0 at Goodison Park. However, the shine was taken off this victory by an untimely injury to Alan Ball. As the powerhouse in their midfield engine room, losing him for an extended period through injury was a bitter blow for the Toffees at a crucial period of the season.

Harry Catterick's reorganisation of his side for the away trip to Southampton was helped by the return from injury of Jimmy Husband and Colin Harvey in the forward line and midfield respectively. However, his decision to play Sandy Brown as a defensive midfield anchor man in front of the back four was a disaster with Southampton taking the points in a 2-1 win, which helped them in their struggle near the bottom of the table. More importantly for Everton, this defeat meant that Leeds United took over at the top of the league. Catterick's team remained in second position as a result of a lack-lustre performance in a 0-0 draw at home to Newcastle United in their next fixture. Even Joe Royle's winner in a 1-0 home win over Wolverhampton Wanderers was not enough to regain top position by the end of the month.

The poor form and results in the Southampton and Newcastle games and being replaced by Leeds United at the top of the league during the absence of Alan Ball had clearly affected team confidence for the first time in the season. This was evident in the atmosphere during first-team training sessions the apprentices caught glimpses of at Bellefield during that period.

Wilf Dixon became noticeably more vocal and demanding as the intensity of the training schedule increased. A seldom-seen tracksuited Harry Catterick appeared more frequently at the side of the training pitch and studied proceedings ever more intently as he and his first-team coach searched for a way to restore Everton's winning edge and with it, their position at the top of the table. It was evident to everyone at the club that things needed to improve.

* * * *

At a time when the fortunes of the first-team were going through a rough patch, I felt my own injury situation was on a similarly poor footing. In spite of following physio Norman Borrowdale's instructions to the letter and receiving the normal regime of heat and ultra sound treatment on my injured ankle, very little noticeable improvement was evident. I was still getting a painful reaction and swelling if I attempted anything other than light jogging or running in a straight line. Towards the end of the month, Mr. Borrowdale was concerned enough about my injury to call in Dr Irving, the club doctor for a second opinion. This was fairly common practice for first-team players who were injured as the club naturally always kept a close eye on the fitness of their prized assets, but it was not usual in the case of apprentices. I was quite flattered and reassured that the club felt the treatment of my injury was important enough to involve the club doctor and was eager to try any recommendations he might make.

During one Dr. Irving's visits to Bellefield, he performed a brief examination of my ankle and asked me to perform a series of agility exercises and describe the pain I was having and what movements caused it. Following a discussion with Mr. Borrowdale about what treatment I had received so far, I was told I had been prescribed a series of electrical stimulation sessions on the ankle for two weeks to strengthen the damaged ligaments. But the doctor said he would need to see me again if the injury did not respond positively.

The electrical stimulation treatment involved a piece of equipment I had not seen Mr. Borrowdale using before. It consisted of a small biscuit tin sized box with a number of switches and dials on the front. From the back of the box, two wires protruded which were attached to two thin silver metal plates about the size of twelve inch rulers. The two metal strips were placed on the floor of the treatment room parallel to one another and about six inches apart. I was instructed to place my foot onto the silver plates – one across the ball of my foot and the other across the heel. When the machine was switched on, a mild electric current passed through the plates for a few seconds causing my foot and ankle muscles to contract and then relax in a fairly comfortable rhythm. However, once the machine had been in operation for a few minutes, Mr. Borrowdale used the dials on the machine to gradually alter both the intensity and the frequency of the convulsions, which was far from comfortable. But to me, the pain and discomfort of the treatment was a small price to pay if it meant regaining my fitness sooner.

In between the two weeks electrical stimulation sessions, I continued to have the usual heat and ultra-sound treatment as well as massage and mobility exercises. Walking, jogging and running circuits were introduced to gradually test out the progress being achieved. This was a very intensive treatment regime and I was really grateful to Mr. Borrowdale for the amount of time and effort he was dedicating to my recovery.

Meanwhile, worryingly for me but positively for Stewart Imlach and the 'B' Team squad, results in January were phenomenal. Five wins out of five against Blackburn Rovers (Home 4-0), Preston North End (Home 8-1), Blackburn Rovers (Away 3-0), Tranmere Rovers (Home 5-1) and Blackpool (Away 3-0) saw them placed near the top of the Lancashire League Division 2. Again I got the feeling of treading water while the rest of the lads continued to develop their skills and fitness along with their reputations with Stewart and Tommy Casey, leaving me further and further behind. The question inevitably entered my mind of how, even when fully fit, I would be able to break back into the 'B' Team when they were on such a good run of results, let alone be considered for promotion to the 'A' Team.

But that particular challenge was for the future. It helped having senior pros like Alan Ball, Colin Harvey and Jimmy Husband in and out of the treatment room at the same time as I was being treated. They all had their own take on how to cope with injuries. Colin Harvey was very supportive saying I should treat it as part of the job and just channel any frustrations into getting full fitness back once the injury was healed. In the absence of any alternative guidance, it seemed the logical thing to do – so that's what I did.

What did worry me though was that Stewart made very little effort to monitor my progress either by popping into the treatment room or in discussion with myself or Mr. Borrowdale. I know he was really busy with the 'B' Team but it seemed to me that the only time he spoke to me, was when another skip load of boots needed cleaning or some other menial task needed to be completed.

My despondency wasn't helped after the two weeks of electrical stimulation treatment recommended by the club doctor was over and there had been no perceivable improvement in my injury. Mr. Borrowdale informed me that, in line with the club doctor's instructions, I was to attend Dr. Irving's private practice in Rodney Street, Liverpool for a consultation about my ankle.

My dad accompanied me for my appointment. I knew Rodney Street was where some of the most eminent private medical practices in the North West of England were situated, but it was my dad who told me how much it would probably cost for a member of the general public to pay for the kind of consultation I was about to receive through Everton FC. Whilst it didn't help my anxiety about being out of action for so long in my first year at the club, it was reassuring to know that Everton were prepared to provide me with the best medical advice and treatment money could buy.

We approached the elegant Georgian townhouse in Rodney Street, climbed the steps to the gleaming black front door to where a highly polished engraved brass plate confirmed we were at the right address and entered into the equally plush and elegant waiting room of Dr. Irving's practice. The receptionist was expecting us and showed us straight into the doctor's consulting room. It was a large airy room with tall sash windows and an ornate ceiling of moulded plasterwork. Not exactly the surroundings my family were used to at Dr. Wallace's surgery on Bewley Drive in Kirkby I thought.

After removing my shoes and socks and changing into a pair of shorts, I was instructed by the doctor to climb onto the treatment table which stood at the far side of the room near an array of medical machines and paraphernalia. Whilst he compared both ankles he massaged, manipulated and bent my ankle inwards until I squirmed with the pain emanating from the outside ligaments. He then got me to do a series of exercises balanced on my injured foot and ankle to assess the mobility in the joint – all of the time noting where I had any pain or discomfort.

Finally after about half-an-hour of exhaustive assessment, Dr. Irving told me to sit down next to my dad.

After washing and drying his hands, he began his feedback about his assessment of my injury.

"I would have expected an injury of the anterior lateral ankle ligaments of this type to have recovered sufficiently for you to be playing again by now, given the length and intensity of the treatment you have had. As far as I see it, there are currently two options for us to consider. Firstly, we could continue with the current treatment regime. But the injury is not responding and continuing indefinitely means that you are losing more valuable time from your apprenticeship with no guarantee of success in the short term. Secondly, and this is my preferred option, I would suggest a series of cortisone injections deep into the injured area. These are extremely painful but the hope would be that the swelling and inflammation in the affected area is curtailed allowing you greater movement and flexibility resulting in a speedier recovery".

He paused for a few moments to allow us to absorb the options he had just outlined for us before adding, "There are risks involved for you whatever option we choose. It depends which gamble you would prefer to take. Ultimately, it's your career and the choice is yours. Which is it to be?"

Dr. Irvine's assessment of my injury and his analysis of the options open to me amplified the feeling I already had of being left behind by the rest of the apprentices the longer I was injured and crystallised how little time I had left to make my mark at Everton and stand any chance of making the grade as a professional footballer. I reasoned that if the cortisone injections, however painful and risky, offered the chance of the quickest return to full fitness, then whatever the odds of success, that was the gamble worth taking. The discussion with my dad was a very brief one.

"Can I have the injections, please", I said emphatically.

The doctor was already preparing a large syringe with a lethal looking three inch needle glistening menacingly at one end.

****

I couldn't believe the difference those injections made to my injury. After a few days the soreness from the area of the injections around the outside of the ankle joint had all but disappeared and the swelling and pain from the ligaments was far less noticeable. Mr. Borrowdale seemed as pleased as I was at the improvement and immediately stepped up the level of training and stamina work I did. Remembering Colin Harvey's advice about channelling any self-doubt and frustrations into regaining fitness after an injury, I put everything I could into every session. By the final week of January, I was re-introduced back into the normal 'B' Team training and coaching sessions and practice matches and after a brief conversation with Stewart Imlach and Tommy Casey, Mr. Borrowdale confirmed that I was fully match fit and available for selection.

I was elated that I had overcome my second injury and was determined to make an impact as soon as I got the opportunity to pull on a royal blue jersey again. I studied the up-coming fixtures for February. First up was the small matter of a mini derby against Liverpool 'B' Team at Bellefield – after the run of form Stewart's team had been on, the sense of anticipation was palpable as these encounters, although between teams from the junior ranks of the Merseyside giants, were always hotly contested.

****

Being deposed by Leeds United at the top of Division 1 may have meant that the odds on Everton winning the title had lengthened but that didn't prevent the first-team players having a flutter at the Bookies whenever there was a tip about a fancied horse doing the rounds. Most of the first-team liked to have a bet from time to time – especially Alan Ball, Colin Harvey and Joe Royle. Betting wasn't banned but it wasn't exactly condoned by Harry Catterick, who presumably saw betting as a distraction from focussing on the next match and two more precious league points.

As a result, all betting activities were carried out in a semi-secretive, almost clandestine atmosphere. As players were unable to leave Bellefield during the day due to the strict time-keeping rules stringently imposed on all players by Harry Catterick, any betting activities had to be organised through a third party or parties. Predictably, Everton's betting third party was none other than that Jack Of all Trades, Sid McGuinness, the assistant groundsman. Not only was Sid the man who placed bets for the players, being a keen horseracing follower, he was also the source of any number of 'hot tips' or 'racing certainties' or so he would have everyone believe.

However, Sid had to overcome one small logistical problem in order to ensure that bets for races at a meeting on any given afternoon were handed to him by lunchtime at the latest so that he could nip out of Bellefield during his dinner break to the nearest Betting Shop in West Derby to place the bets. That's where myself and one or two of the other apprentices came in. As soon as the players had studied their morning papers and decided on their selections for the day, we would be sent over to Sid's shed with their hastily scribbled bets and the appropriate amount of cash for him to put the bets on. This had to be done in a furtive and secretive way in order not to arouse the suspicions of Mr. Catterick or any of the coaching staff if they were in the vacinity.

Having been injured and in and out of the treatment room at the same time as both Alan Ball and Colin Harvey, I got to know their preferred bets and what 'tips' Sid had let them have and was invariably the one they entrusted to do their betting business. Sid was, however, sometimes the victim of his own success or otherwise as a tipster. At one Haydock Park meeting, he had enthused about an 'absolute racing certainty' that was running in the 3.30 race. Most of the regular gamblers duly placed a fair amount of cash onto his tip and, as training had finished early for the afternoon, Sid and most of the senior players crowded around a tiny transistor radio in the first-team changing room to listen to the commentary. Sid's 'certainty' trailed in last amidst a barrage of abuse from his 'clients' after which he was hoisted aloft and dumped head first into one of the freezing water plunge-baths in the shower area, where he was left to coldly reflect on his expertise as a tipster.

* * * *

Being the go-between for Alan Ball and Colin Harvey wasn't my only experience of carrying bets to Bookies' Runners. My dad was a keen, if not very talented horse fancier, who regularly spent time scouring the racing pages of the Daily Mirror and the Racing Post. In Kirkby at the time there wasn't the luxury of an actual Betting Shop for the punters to indulge their passion for a flutter. My dad and his betting pals, who congregated in the Kingfisher Public House in Southdene, had to make do with a Bookies Runner, who went by the name of Wally.

Wally was a squat, roly-poly, florid-faced man in his fifties who gave the impression of being as wide as he was tall. Always wearing a stained, shiny, threadbare suit, he would wait in the small, narrow entrance foyer which separated the main entrance of the pub from the double doors leading to the smoky public bar. Punters would approach Wally with their bets scribbled onto any scrap of paper they could lay their hands on and give them to him amid furtive glances from Wally from out of the pub entrance doors in case any of the police cars that regularly cruised the Kirkby streets happened upon him and his unlicensed and illegal operation. Each gambler had their own unique pseudonym or set of initials. My dad's was E.L.O. for Edward Leslie Osborne and Wally used these to identify the punters he had to pay out in the event of them placing a winning bet with him.

On some occasions, Wally was prepared to accept a bet a minute or so after the official time of the start of the race, especially if it was delivered by myself or either of my brothers Alan or Eddie, sweaty and out of breath because my dad was late in writing his bet out and made us sprint around to place it for him. As soon as Wally saw the E.L.O. initials of one of his most profitable clients, he was happy to place it with the wad of bets he had already received and put my dad's hard-earned cash with the fat roll of notes in his bulging jacket pocket.

Quite by chance, around that time, our Alan had acquired a pair of hand held walkie-talkie wireless radios, which we amused ourselves with, in and around Alford Road and the Southdene area of Kirkby in general. Being of an enterprising nature and creative thinkers, it wasn't long before we hatched a plan to use the walkie-talkies to relieve Wally of some of the cash my Dad had furnished him with over the years. We'd worked out that if Wally was prepared to accept a bet after the official start time of a race, we might be able to get the result of a short five furlong race while watching on TV and use the walkie-talkies to get the name of the winner to one of us who would be waiting at the rear of the Kingfisher to scribble it down and run round to Wally and place the winning bet using my dad's pseudonym 'E. L. O.'

Sadly, our plan never amounted to much due to a variety of circumstances; either the range of the walkie-talkies wasn't wide enough to cover the distance from our house to the Kingfisher meaning the result could only be sent half-way and after writing the result down, it took too long to get to Wally to place the bet; or there was too much interference and we couldn't recognise the name of the winner on the handset anyway. Even when we got clear reception and got our timing to perfection, Wally wouldn't accept the bet saying we were too late. We suspected our scam had been exposed to Wally by someone who knew what we were up to and we decided that our fledgling foray into the murky world of illegal betting was never going to be a winner - each way we looked at it.

FEBRUARY 1970
TAKING THE PEE

On paper, February's first-team fixtures appeared to provide a golden opportunity for Everton to recapture their championship pole position by leapfrogging above Leeds United to the top of Division 1. Having exited early from both domestic cup competitions, a relatively light programme of just three league fixtures for the month presented Harry Catterick's team with two home games against Arsenal and then Coventry City followed by an away match versus Nottingham Forest. All three teams had been experiencing fairly mundane mid-table campaigns and most of the press coverage backed Everton to take full advantage in a reinvigorated challenge for the title.

However, the mood of optimism which was apparent around Bellefield at the start of the month soon evaporated as Arsenal held the Toffees to a 2-2 draw in spite of two goals from Alan Whittle who was continuing to make the most of his first extended run in the first-team as a replacement for Jimmy Husband and Alan Ball. Further disappointments as a result of a goal-less draw against Coventry City at a subdued Goodison Park and only securing a point in a 1-1 draw in Nottingham had eroded the atmosphere at Bellefield and had even the calm, measured and confident Wilf Dixon and Harry Catterick showing signs of tension.

Normal Monday mornings at Bellefield consisted of the players reporting at the allotted time for training and changing in their respective dressing rooms and waiting to be called for their pre-training warm-up. The apprentices were usually popping in and out of the pros' dressing rooms with towels, items of missing kit or boots after running repairs and re-studding had been completed.

The Monday morning after the Nottingham Forest game was to be very different. Stewart Imlach and Tommy Casey had come into the apprentices early to tell us that under no circumstances were we to go into the first-team dressing room because training was starting late due to Harry Catterick and

Wilf Dixon convening a meeting of the senior squad. Naturally, we were all intrigued as to the reason such a meeting would be taking place and why we were warned so strictly not to interrupt.

We concluded that it must be to do with the run of less than impressive draws which had stalled Everton's title challenge during February. Whilst it was almost certainly an accurate assumption, our curiosity got the better of us and we decided to draw lots to see who would go and loiter outside the first-team dressing room to glean any snippets of information or gossip about proceedings within. In the absence of straws we used lengths of cut up boot laces to draw lots and I was the unfortunate soul who drew the shortest and was assigned to my dangerous and nerve-wracking spying mission. So, armed with a bundle of fresh towels and a flimsy excuse about being asked for them earlier, I sidled along the corridor towards where I could hear raised voices growing ever louder with each step. As I approached the first-team dressing room, I could clearly hear Harry Catterick and Wilf Dixon remonstrating intermittently with the senior players about the recent poor results and performances and where it left the club and their chances of lifting the league trophy at the end of the season. No individual players were singled out in what was primarily a whole-squad rollicking.

I nearly dropped my bundle of towels as the meeting reached its climax when the door burst open and an incandescent Harry Catterick emerged before he rounded on his players and retorted, "And if you think that sort of performance is going to win us the league, then you lot have got another thing coming!"

He then brushed past me, hardly noticing I was there, adding under his breath, "They're taking the piss!"

Wilf Dixon followed, silently glowering in Mr. Catterick's wake, leaving a stunned and chastened first-team squad to reflect on the thoughts and home truths provided for them by their manager and coach. As I edged nervously back towards the apprentice's dressing room to report back having accomplished my mission, only one voice could be heard. It was that of club captain, Brian Labone, whose words had the ring of truth about them when he said, "Lads, I can't disagree with a word of that. The Boss and Wilf are right and they're doing their bit – the rest is up to us. We've got a responsibility to this club and to our fans. Now do we want to win this league or what?"

The response from the dressing room made it very clear that they most certainly did.

****

Although I was approaching full match fitness following my ankle injury and had been back in training with Stewart and the 'B' Team, I supposed it was too much to hope for a return straight into the team for the mini-derby against Liverpool, especially as they had swept all before them with five straight wins in January. And that was how things panned out. With the 'A' Team having no fixture, naturally Stewart selected some of the eligible players from Tommy Casey's 'A' Team to strengthen his side for this keenly awaited clash of the clubs' junior sides at Bellefield. Sadly for me, it was no surprise that it meant no place for me in the squad and I had to sit it out alongside Peter Whitwood and one or two other apprentices.

What was a surprise was the result. Stewart was not best pleased when the Liverpool 'B' Team ran out comfortable 2-0 winners, when a resounding victory for the Blues was confidently predicted given Everton's recent run of results in the Lancashire League and the strength of the team Stewart selected. The one crumb of comfort to come out of this for me was that a poor result against Liverpool meant that there was a greater chance of me being considered for one or both of the remaining two fixtures in February. It was selfish I know, but I was so desperate to be playing again that I was half hoping for Stewart's team to have poor results without me so that he would be almost forced to give me the starting place I was craving for.

Frustratingly, I was not selected for either of the other games in February against Crewe Alexandra and Tranmere Rovers. In fact, the harder I tried to impress Stewart in training, the more he ignored me. It seemed on occasions that he was even trying to force me out of the arrangements on match days when I wasn't playing. For example he even told me to leave the dressing room before the team talk prior to the kick off. Instead I was told to take kicking in balls to the opposing team rather than being kept involved with preparation as a squad member.

I even had difficulty persuading Stewart that I needed new boots. The system was for apprentices to have two pairs of boots – one pair for training and their best pair for matches. As the training boots were prone to wear out very quickly due to daily use, new boots were allocated by the coach if he deemed them to be beyond repair. The new boots were usually broken in during training for a week or so, to be used as match boots with the old match boots being relegated to be used as training boots. My training boots were in a right state having been repaired twice and I showed them to Stewart on a number of occasions but he refused to replace them with a new pair while other apprentices seemed to have little difficulty in securing a new pair from either him or Tommy Casey.

This situation came to a head one afternoon when we were doing a shooting practice drill where Stewart had arranged for us to play the ball from the centre circle to the edge of the penalty box where the 'target man' would lay the ball off into our path to run onto and finish past the goalkeeper. It must have been a quiet afternoon for the first-team because Wilf Dixon happened to be watching casually from the touchline as he sometimes did. Things were going well until after one shot, my right boot finally gave up the ghost and split with the sole coming adrift from the upper from the toe to the instep and began to flap around like a flipper. As a result I floundered about with my boot half on and half off and missed my turn in the shooting drill as I tried to fathom what had happened, to which Stewart shouted, "Come on man, it's your turn. Get a move on!"

Angered by the state of my boots and embarrassed that what had happened had been witnessed by the first-team coach, I shouted back, "How can I Stewart with the state of these frigging boots? What do I have to do to get a new pair? Play in bare feet? It's taking the piss!"

With that I flip-flopped to the side of the pitch and removed my mangled boot before waddling off to find a replacement from amongst a box of discarded oddments of right boots in the boot room. Steward looked sheepishly in the direction of Wilf Dixon who was already making his way back to the dressing rooms. I don't know whether it was my remonstration with Stewart or if Wilf Dixon had a quiet word with Stewart, but the following morning a brand new pair of Adidas Santiago were in my place in the apprentices' dressing room when I arrived for training. I finally got my new boots, but sadly, Stewart didn't see fit for me to wear them in an Everton 'B' Team game for the rest of the month.

Being out of the team when fully fit brought home the frustrations I was feeling. Having been at Everton for eight months and having two periods out of action due to injuries highlighted the progress my peers in the 1969 intake of apprentices had made. Ray Pritchard and Paul McEwan my Kirkby counterparts had made several appearances for Tommy Casey's 'A' Team alongside Liverpool Boys' Ronny Goodlass and Manchester lad Mick Buckley joining them. Only myself and Peter Whitwood had failed to progress beyond the 'B' Team due mainly to injury for myself but due to loss of confidence and form for Peter.

****

If competition for places on the pitch was fierce, it was no less competitive around Bellefield both in and out of training sessions. The fact that Everton had begun to recruit players from Kirkby Schoolboys as well as Liverpool Schoolboys over the past two years added a little spice to training sessions. The pro ranks of Everton were scattered with ex-Liverpool Schoolboys who had been snapped up through the Everton scouting system. Players like Joe Royle, Colin Harvey, Tommy Wright had all made their way to the club via that particular route and it was almost the norm for a handful Liverpool Schoolboys to be spotted and signed each year. What had changed over the past couple of years was that the emergence of Kirkby Schools F.A. as a force locally meant there was competition on Merseyside both in the schoolboy ranks and within the clubs they signed for.

There was always an edge in training if ever the ex-Liverpool lads were pitted against the ex-Kirkby lads and myself, Ray Pritchard, Paul McEwan,

The changing room and bath area at Bellefield

Peter Scott and Keith Williams were always up for the challenge on the pitch against the likes of Ronny Goodlass, Ian Bacon, Joe Moran, John Smith and Alan Wilson. But the Liverpool-Kirkby rivalry did get out of hand occasionally.

On one occasion after the morning training session, I climbed down into one of the large plunge baths which was always invitingly half filled with warm soapy water for bathing. Most of the apprentices had already bathed and only ex-Liverpool lads Joe Moran, Alan Wilson and John Smith were left in the bath.

"How long can you hold your breath under water for Stan?" asked Joe Moran. "Don't know, why?" was my curious reply.

"We're just having a competition. Do you want to have a go?" Alan enquired. Now being the only Kirkby lad amongst the four of us, I wasn't about to be seen to back down.

"Alright, I'll have a go", I said confidently.

"OK, we'll go first", said John Smith, eager to launch the underwater challenge as he proceeded to duck, face down in the water, with the others counting rhythmically to 25 when he emerged gasping for air.

I failed to be impressed by John's performance and remained confident in my ability to stave off the Liverpool challenge when Alan and Joe only managed 30 and 35 seconds respectively. With that, all three invited me to beat their best time. So after a couple of deep breaths, I submerged my face into the warm water and carefully counted to myself up to 30 seconds, then to 40 and on to 60 to make sure I'd passed their best time comfortably. However, just as I had reached the 60 second mark, I became aware of a hot stream running from the back of my head, down my face towards my mouth and I sensed a strong salty taste in the water. Raising my head from the bath water, I emerged to howls of hysterical laughter as all of the apprentices circled the bath watching as Joe, John and Alan stood pissing on my head having tricked me into their underwater challenge.

I went absolutely ballistic chasing all three of them out of the bathing area, through the apprentices' dressing room and down the corridor, cracking a wet towel off their arses as they fled. As we reached the end of the corridor, to our horror, the Trainers Dressing Room door opened and Harry Catterick appeared and was nearly knocked off his feet by four dripping wet naked apprentices. As we stood silently trying to hide our embarrassment and awaiting admonishment, Catterick fixed his steely glare into each of our faces as if memorising us individually and then said calmly, "That's not what you get paid for. Get your kit on and see Stewart Imlach outside in five minutes!"

He then disappeared back into the Trainers Dressing Room presumably to instruct Stewart as to how he wished us to be disciplined. Half an hour later, after a series of exhausting sprints, shuttles and laps of the training pitch, we collapsed back into the warm plunge bath water. But this time there was no pissing about!

At the time, Mr. Catterick's harsh disciplining of us after our underwater exploits seemed a bit over the top for what was basically high jinks amongst the youngsters that, earlier in the season, when Everton were riding high at the top of Division One, might have been laughed off. However, it did reflect the much sterner approach being adopted throughout the club as the league programme for the first-team was reaching its concluding months and the chance to lift the League Title remained tantalisingly close.

MARCH 1970
TOP OF THE WORLD MA!

Clearly the anxiety and tensions felt around Bellefield and the uncharacteristically abrasive episodes which resulted, meant a good run of league results was essential during March if the atmosphere was to improve and with it Everton's challenge for the title. Looking at the fixtures for the month, it wasn't going to be easy for Harry Catterick's men. Six games awaited them over a period of just 23 days – four of which were away from Goodison Park including a trip across Stanley Park for the return derby match against Liverpool at Anfield. It was obvious that these matches would largely determine where the league title would end up on April 8th. Both the manager and his coach, Wilf Dixon must have been hoping that the 'clear the air' meeting they held with the senior players at the end of February and the increasingly demanding training regime would produce a reaction on the pitch and a resultant improvement in their form and results.

So it was with great trepidation, but encouraged by the return of Alan Ball from injury, that the hoards of Evertonians made the short trip across Lancashire to Turf Moor for the opening fixture of the month against Burnley. In a nervy encounter, goals from Alan Ball and John Hurst sent the Toffees' fans back Merseyside with smiles on their faces as Everton secured both points in a 2-1 win. They followed this up the following Wednesday evening with an impressive 1-0 victory at White Hart Lane against Tottenham Hotspur thanks to a goal from Alan Whittle in the match that was rearranged from December due to floodlight failure. This created a strange anomaly in the fixtures, meaning Spurs visited Goodison Park three days later for the return fixture and, in a thrilling encounter witnessed by over 51,000, Everton made it a hat trick of wins with a 3-2 victory, the goals coming from Alan Ball (pen), Joe Royle and, again, a crucial one from Alan Whittle.

Confidence was coursing through the team again thanks to the run of three wins out of three. This set up the mouth-watering prospect of

Everton visiting Anfield in their next match needing a win, not only to avenge the humiliating 3-0 defeat at Goodison at the hands of their neighbours in December, but with the chance to regain the lead in the race for the championship from Leeds United with only five matches remaining.

The Anfield derby was to prove a tactical triumph for Harry Catterick, providing a pivotal point in the whole season. In front of an expectant Kop, Everton played superbly and with Alan Whittle playing off the aerial threat of Joe Royle, Liverpool could not cope with his pace as Royle broke the deadlock and Whittle skipped past a floundering Liverpool defence to seal the match. Just as Bill Shankly had masterminded his side's victory at Goodison, Harry Catterick had fashioned a plan to unpick the Liverpool defence. As they secured two more precious points, Gordon West, the Everton goalie, having endured merciless barracking from the Liverpool fans all afternoon, provided an iconic moment when he celebrated the victory facing a stunned Kop, which sent the visiting Everton fans into raptures. There could have been no better place to be for Evertonians than a Liverpool pub on that Saturday evening. Their team were top of the league and they must have felt on top of the world.

The momentum being generated by Everton was proving unstoppable as on the following Saturday they entertained highly placed Chelsea at Goodison Park. 58,000 supporters squeezed into the ground to witness what they hoped would be another step towards the League Championship. Chelsea were to prove no match for a superb Everton who swept them aside in a 5-2 win, which included two goals from Joe Royle, one each from Alan Ball and Howard Kendall with Alan Whittle scoring in his fourth game in succession.

Everton completed a clean sweep of wins in all six matches in March, when they overcame Stoke City in a tricky away fixture at the Victoria Ground thanks to Alan Whittle's fifth goal of the month. This left Everton sitting proudly at the top of the league with the final three fixtures of the season to be played in the first eight days of April.

In the space of those 23 March days in which they had strung together a spectacular sequence of results, Harry Catterick had used all his experience, skill and guile to cajole, motivate and inspire his players to recapture their early season form and mount a challenge that had their main challengers trailing in their wake. It was now going to take a brave man to put his money on any other team than Everton winning the title.

****

As the season unfolded and the prospect of another League Championship emerged, it was inevitable that Everton players figured prominently in England Manager Alf Ramsey's plans during the build up to their defence of the World Cup in Mexico during the summer of 1970.

Liverpool 0 Everton 2 – Gordon West celebrates in front of the Kop

As a key member of the triumphant 1966 England team, Alan Ball was considered an automatic choice in midfield. When Ramsey announced his squad in March 1970, Alan Ball was joined by Everton team-mates, centre-half and captain, Brian Labone and full backs Tommy Wright and Keith Newton. It was surprising to many Evertonians that Colin Harvey and Howard Kendall were not included in the England set-up, bearing in mind their almost telepathic understanding with Alan Ball in Everton's talismanic midfield that season.

But even more of a puzzle to everyone was Gordon West's decision to write to Alf Ramsey asking not to be included in the England squad that would be travelling to Mexico. With over twenty clean sheets to his name so far and some outstanding and consistent performances in Everton's goal, he was widely considered to be the natural choice as understudy to Gordon Banks for the World Cup tournament.

There were a number of theories which circulated within the club at the time regarding his decision. Firstly, there were rumours about Gordon having weight problems. This theory carried little credibility though as, along with the rest of the Everton squad, he was fully fit and having his weight carefully monitored in training where he was working hard as the club pushed towards hopefully securing the league title. Secondly, there was his nervous temperament, which was largely contained and overcome as Everton 'keeper'. However, it was suggested in some quarters that the prospect of being under the world spotlight with the hopes of the nation resting on his shoulders had an influence on his decision.

There was also a third theory about why Gordon didn't want to be in the England squad for Mexico. This was to do with him wanting to spend more time at home with his family. At the time, Gordon went public in a statement, which was published in the match day programme for the league fixture against Southampton. He stated that, after a full league campaign with Everton, he couldn't give of his best for England and wanted to spend his close season with his wife and family. The statement, though, did not put an end to the speculation – or the stick he got from the other members of the first-team squad!

All of this was a side issue to us apprentices, who enjoyed the reflected glory that Everton being at the top of the league and having four players named in the England World Cup Squad brought to the club. The dour atmosphere that had pervaded the training ground during a difficult January and February had been replaced by a far more relaxed and optimistic outlook following the outstanding run of results in March.

One additional bonus for Everton's four England World Cup players was that they were each allocated a brand new Ford Cortina 1600E as part of Ford's sponsorship of the England team. Amid a huge publicity launch, each of Alf Ramsey's squad was presented with the keys of the new cars and were filmed and photographed by TV companies and the national press as part of the build-up to the World Cup tournament. The players had exclusive use of the cars up to the World Cup after which the cars had to be returned to Fords. In exchange Fords benefited from the publicity that having the country's best footballers driving their most prestigious model around was sure to bring.

The arrival of Alan Ball, Brian Labone, Tommy Wright and Keith Newton in their new Fords was keenly anticipated at Bellefield and they caused quite a stir when they arrived in the car park before training one day with everyone giving them the once over. They were lovely cars with gleaming metallic paintwork, leather upholstery, sports wheels and glistening chrome trim. The distinctive growl of the sporty 1600E Ford engines meant all the pros where eager to have a turn behind the wheel.

The bonus for us apprentices was that, as part of the sponsorship deal, the England players had to attend a number of official Ford Motor Company publicity events sporting their Cortina 1600E's. As the cars did not actually belong to the players and with footballers not exactly being enthusiastic about getting their hands dirty by cleaning their motors, we made a few extra pounds to supplement our apprentices wages by cleaning them ready for these functions. It also gave us the opportunity to indulge our fantasies by sitting in the driver's seat with the stereo playing, imagining we were one of Everton players in the England squad that would be heading to Mexico at the end of the season...... If only.

****

Sadly, the optimism surrounding Bellefield didn't extend to my own playing prospects. I felt as though I was back to full fitness and having no adverse reaction to my ankle injury after training or in full scale practice matches. I was confident that Stewart would be considering me for selection soon and continued to put all my efforts into training – so much so that my enthusiasm in the tackle during five-a-side matches was sometimes overstated resulting in more than one unseemly fracas as the competitive edge amongst the apprentices surfaced. I'd made my mind up that there was no way I was going to back down if there was a challenge to be made on the basis that it would only be perceived by the lads, the coaches or the opposing team as a sign of weakness. From now on for me it was going to be 'full steam ahead' and hang the consequences if anyone got in the way.

I think the penny had finally dropped for me, albeit belatedly, and I had realised that nobody at Everton – players or coaches - was going to do me any favours and that looking after yourself was what mattered if you were going to survive and stand any chance of making the grade as a player.

Part of the reason for the hardening of my attitude was down to the way I had been largely ignored by Stewart Imlach during my injuries and then overlooked and marginalised by him since my return to fitness. Another factor was the way Peter Whitwood had fared since he joined the club as an apprentice at the same time as me. Being from Essex, he was a prime target for all the mickey taking and pranks and his confidence had plunged when he was the victim of the infamous 'court case' early in his apprenticeship. His morale and spirits were at such a low ebb that after a number of conversations between Peter, his parents and the club, he decided to leave and move back home to Grays. Basically, he was a long way from home, had found life in digs hard while dealing with the demands of his sport and basically had been unable to cope with life as an apprentice. I was determined that I was going to do all I could not to experience the same fate, deciding instead to come out fighting – literally if necessary.

I was to be given one more chance by Stewart in the 'B' Team in March, however that was more due to unforeseen circumstances than his preference. When the team-sheet went up for the match away to Burnley, it confirmed that I had not been selected, but was named to travel with the squad. I was infuriated that three trialists had been selected ahead of me and would be making their own way to the Burnley training ground as they were from that part of Lancashire. For whatever reason, the trialists did not arrive at the Burnley training ground, leaving Stewart with just ten players at his disposal. He had no alternative but to reluctantly tell me I would be playing centre forward and was also forced to name himself in the starting line-up.

It was strange having your coach playing in the same side. Stewart was still a very skilful and tricky winger as you would have expected given his Nottingham Forest and Scotland international pedigree. However, I and the other apprentices didn't miss the opportunity to give him a mild bollocking if he misplaced a pass or made a mistake. I ran myself into the ground, realising that I needed to make the most of this unexpected opportunity to pull on an Everton shirt again and impress upon Stewart that I was fully committed to working myself back into his plans. I felt as if I had a reasonable game and was pleased to open the scoring and afterwards leave the pitch exhausted and delighted with a comfortable 4-1 win.

After the match, whilst not expecting any individual praise for myself, I would have expected Stewart at least to have congratulated the team for securing a good result in unusual circumstances given the non-arrival of the trialists. But apart from a fairly trite, "Well played, lads", there was very little by way of a debrief or feedback about our performance and we settled down to a fairly subdued coach journey back to Merseyside.

If my hopes had been raised that my impromptu appearance in the 'B' Team might have heralded further selection in the remaining three scheduled fixtures of the season, they were to be short lived as it was back to 'business as usual' as far as Stewart's attitude towards me was concerned.

That was to be my last game of the season and I was left to ponder whether my worst fears were to be realised and it was to be my last game for the club ever as I wrestled with self-doubt that my injuries and non-selection had created. Stewart's handling of me had convinced me that he did not rate me as a player and that he would prefer it if I left at the end of the season with 18 months still left on my contract and was replaced as one of Everton's 15 apprentices.

* * * *

If I was down in the dumps while Everton and their World Cup players were on top of the world, my spirits were raised one Friday afternoon when I returned home to Kirkby after training at Bellefield. As I turned the corner into Aldford Road, I was met with the unusual sight of quite a crowd of the local kids congregating outside our house.

Even more unusually my older brother Eddie, having returned for the weekend from his job working for the Forestry Commission in North Wales, had decided to demonstrate some of his mountaineering skills to the neighbours. He was a keen walker and climber and for a time was a member of the Ogwen Valley Mountain Rescue Team in Snowdonia.

He had managed to lasso his climbing rope around the chimney stack of our house and was practicing his abseiling down the front of the building to cheers and applause from the gathering of local kids. He even offered to teach some of them the rudiments of abseiling until my mum came out the house and remonstrated with him for his antics, to which he replied, "Top of the world, Ma! Top of the world!"

"James Cagney, eat your heart out", I thought.

APRIL 1970
CHAMPIONS

Everton's irresistible charge back to the top League Division 1 on the back of a remarkable run of six successive victories during March left them with a virtually unassailable lead in the race to be crowned champions. There were three matches of the season remaining, which had to be played in the space of eight days at the beginning of April. The first of these fixtures was the Toffees' only remaining one at home, on the 1st April, but the press weren't fooling any Evertonians when some reports speculated that Leeds United might still launch a late bid to clinch the title. In fact the bookies made Everton hot favourites to lift the trophy at that home match with a win against West Bromwich Albion on the Wednesday evening.

So the stage was set on a warm spring evening under the floodlights at Goodison Park for Harry Catterick's team to seal the points that could deliver Everton Football Club their second championship under his management.

Preparations for the match went smoothly on the morning of the match as the first-team squad had a light training session and massage before meeting with Mr. Catterick and coach Wilf Dixon in the Players' Lounge for a pre-match tactical meeting before lunch. The rest of the playing staff trained as normal in the morning with the pros being dismissed after their lunch, being told to report for their complimentary tickets to watch what was potentially the championship deciding match at Goodison.

Needless to say, the apprentices had to make their way to Goodison to ensure that all the first-team's boots were cleaned and prepared for the match. As luck would have it, a number of the first-team were going to Goodison to drop off their cars at the car park to the rear of the Park End Stand and I was happy to pile into Howard Kendall's Jag with about six others for the short trip from Bellefield.

By four o'clock in the Home Dressing Room, the boots were cleaned and checked, the kit laid out, the match and kicking-in balls pumped up and all the other minor tasks completed to Wilf Dixon's satisfaction and we were dismissed to return at six o'clock to attend to any last minute details of preparation.

Some of the lads who lived more locally to the ground went home, but I decided to stay at Goodison as a trip all the way back to Kirkby would have meant that it would have been difficult to get back before the allotted time given that all public transport was going to be crammed with fans heading to the match.

In any case I loved being at Goodison Park! Ever since I was a kid I used to imagine what it was like for the players under the stand in the dressing room before the kick-off to another Everton match and then walking down the tunnel and up onto the pitch to the crescendo of noise as the theme to 'Z Cars' threaded its way through the roar of the crowd as the teams emerged. Now I had the chance to find out. In the couple of hours before we were due to report back, I wandered around the still-to-be-completed new Main Stand where the new changing facilities were and soaked in the atmosphere. I walked down the tunnel that leads the teams to the pitch and climbed the steps onto the cinder path surrounding the vividly green closely mown grass.

The floodlights were already on and stewards and ground staff were busily completing last minute duties prior to the turnstiles being opened to admit the crowds of avid Evertonians eager for their team to deliver the championship trophy they deserved. I looked left to the Gwladys Street terrace where I used to stand, then right to the Park End Stand before catching a glimpse of the first spectators making their way to their seats in the Bullens Road Stand, which stood imposingly opposite the players tunnel.

Behind me the huge structure that formed the new Main Stand towered over St Luke's Church at its one end, where it stood as it always had; a silent red-brick sentry ready to witness every moment of the match as it unfolded. Goodison Park bedecked in blue and white stood proud and expectant – a worthy arena for such an auspicious occasion. It felt good to be an Evertonian.

As I returned towards the Home Dressing Room, through the Player's Entrance door, I caught glimpses of Goodison Road already packed with Everton fans making their way to or from The Winslow or The Spellow or maybe The Chepstow Castle on County Road – any of the multitude of pubs around Goodison Park where a nerve-calming pint could be found and enjoyed with fellow Blues as the build-up to the kick-off approached.

When I got to the Home Dressing Room at six o'clock, most of the other apprentices were there. A calm and collected Wilf Dixon was sending apprentices on errands for odd bits of equipment. The room looked resplendent with the royal blue shirts and white shorts and socks hanging patiently waiting to be donned by the players. Spotless boots stood on the floor below each kit, with blue towels neatly folded on the benches above. Two massage tables standing side by side in the middle of the room completed the picture as we waited for the players to arrive.

The quiet calm of the dressing room was soon replaced by the growing hubbub of conversations, wise-cracks and banter as the players arrived and began changing into their kit, filling the room with an air of anticipation as kick-off time slowly approached.

As we tended to any last-minute tasks, it was interesting to observe how the players interacted and went through their pre-match rituals. Alan Ball was his usual exuberant self, chattering away in high pitched, enthused excitement to a confident and assured Joe Royle. This contrasted markedly with Gordon West who was suffering from his normal bout of nerves before a match. He paced up and down wringing his hands and taking deep breaths before disappearing intermittently into the bathing and toilet area from where the sound of retching could be heard.

Club Captain, Brian Labone, although not playing due to injury, strode purposefully around the room with a steadying word for the nervous looking Alan Whittle and an encouraging bit of advice for his own replacement at centre half, the talented but inexperienced Roger Kenyon. Howard Kendall, Johnny Morrissey, Tommy Wright and Colin Harvey, calm and collected as you like, looked as if they were getting changed for a practice match, while John Hurst and Sandy Brown, who was replacing the injured Keith Newton, were a silent and brooding presence in the corner.

Manager, Harry Catterick was a peripheral figure moving around the edge of the room, remaining silent except for the odd word or comment to individual players. A quiet aside to Gordon West seemed to settle his nerves as did encouraging comments to Alan Whittle and Roger Kenyon.

With about half an hour to go to kick-off, we apprentices were dismissed to take up our seats in the Main Stand as Wilf Dixon called for the players' attention as he and Harry Catterick began their final briefing for this young Everton side before kick-off. As the door closed behind us, it was with a confident stride that we all made our way to our places in the Goodison cauldron that was coming nicely to the boil as the kick-off approached.

Predictably, Goodison Park was a firmament of anticipation until the first strains of 'Z Cars' were drowned out by a crescendo of voices, songs and chants, which layered over each other to produce an ear-splitting roar that reverberated from end to end of the ground and only subsided as the teams lined up for the kick-off.

Bellowed on by a rabidly partisan following, Everton dominated the early exchanges but were being frustrated by a well organised West Brom side, who had John Osborne in control of Everton's aerial threat as he punched clear several crosses, which were aimed at the head of Joe Royle. After about 20 minutes Everton nerves were beginning to show until Alan Whittle showed lightening quick reactions to latch onto to the ball in the penalty area and finish expertly, rifling the ball into the West Brom goal to send the home crowd delirious.

Everton were in complete control now but West Brom were presenting a threat on the break and it wasn't until the 65 minutes mark that the result was put beyond doubt when Colin Harvey fired a superb effort into the roof of the visitors' net, which sent Goodison into rapturous celebration.

The deafening pandemonium continued long after the final whistle blew and stand-in captain Alan Ball was presented with the League Trophy before a triumphant and adoring Goodison Park on an evening that would live long in the memory of all the 58,000 who were lucky enough to be there to witness it.

Everton were League Champions for the seventh time and no one could deny it was utterly deserved.

* * * *

Goodison was still reverberating with the celebrations of the fans when we were eventually able to get back into the Home Dressing Room. Once the well-wishers, press and radio interviewers had dispersed slightly, the apprentices managed to squeeze through the door amid scenes of post-match celebration. We dodged flying champagne corks as we tried as best we could to collect the kit and towels ready to take to the laundry room. Apart from Harry Catterick and the whole of the playing and coaching staff, the room was packed with assorted VIP's and Board Members. As mere apprentices, we were largely ignored as we attempted to go about our duties as anonymously as we could.

As the drinks flowed and the cameras flashed, we eventually cleared the last of the post-match debris, then stood around the edge of the dressing room feeling like uninvited guests at a wedding reception. As we did so, we felt the warm reflected glow of the club's success but although we were immersed in the seductive aura of the occasion, we didn't actually feel part of it.

It was then that Brian Labone made a small but very important gesture.

Dressed in his immaculate suit and matching club tie, he trawled around the dressing room picking up each champagne bottle he could find and gauged the contents of each one, putting any that weren't empty near his place. One of the other players challenged him saying," Hey Labby, you're not thinking of having that lot for yourself are you?"

Brian smiled and replied, "Don't worry, there's plenty left for you".

He then pointed to the assembled apprentices and said, "These lads haven't had a chance to celebrate yet. Get yourselves over here lads and have a drink".

He then proceeded to pour every one of us a glass of champagne and insisted that everyone in the room joined us in a toast to Everton Football Club.

I was the last one to receive my drink, which coincidentally was the last one from the bottle. Brian handed me the empty champagne bottle and said, "Keep hold of that and every time you look at it remember tonight and remember just how special Everton Football Club is".

Delighted with my gift from the club captain, I borrowed a pen and went around the dressing room asking the players, Mr. Catterick and Wilf Dixon to autograph the label to make it a treasured memento from a unique night in the club's history.

Brian Labone's gesture to me and my fellow apprentices meant a great deal to us. Having spent the entire season doing the unglamorous behind the scenes jobs, it meant a lot to everyone to be acknowledged in that way and spoke volumes about the kind of person he was.

****

Having secured the Title, Everton completed their fixtures with a 1-0 away win at Sheffield Wednesday and a midweek goal-less draw away to Sunderland on 8th April. An extraordinary run of results meant they finished the season at the end of a 14 match unbeaten sequence, which stretched back to January and saw them drop only five league points in the process. The Championship was secured by a nine point margin over FA Cup Finalists Leeds United and, more importantly for Evertonians, a 15 point lead over Liverpool.

The season was rightly seen as a triumph of Harry Catterick's management and the culmination of the rebuilding of his squad since Everton's last title in 1963. He had skilfully knitted together the remnants of that team with new high profile signings like Alan Ball and successfully established a youth policy that had become hugely successful in nurturing and developing a string of top flight players and future internationals. All of this was overseen and supported by a Chairman and Board of Directors with a long-term vision for the club and the resources to invest in the team and the ground in order to keep in the vanguard of the English game.

Evertonians revelled in the success Catterick had brought – two League Titles, an FA Cup and an FA Cup Runners-up spot in the space of seven years. And all achieved playing with a style and flair that had become synonymous with Everton's School of Science traditions. A young squad with an average age of under 25 had been assembled and every Everton supporter looked forward to the manager building a dynasty that would bring more and more silverware to the blue half of Merseyside.

****

At the end of the 1969/70 Season, the contrast between the euphoria surrounding Everton's seventh League Title and gloom pervading my own career couldn't have been more stark.

It was a natural juncture at which to pause, reflect and take stock of what had or hadn't been achieved. In my first season as an apprentice, which started with such high hopes, I had achieved a personal ambition of playing for Everton but had suffered the frustration of two lengthy periods out of the game due to injury. Having worked to get back to full fitness, I was basically marginalised by 'B' Team coach Stewart Imlach, who had made it clear in his handling of me that he didn't rate me as a player and would prefer it if I left the club.

When I looked at the figures, it was easy to see why Stewart might have formed that opinion. I had played just nine matches all season, scoring four goals. However, I was fit and available for a further 15 or so matches but was not selected, often with trailists being preferred to myself or some of the other apprentices. It seemed ludicrous to me that Everton were paying apprentices full-time wages only for the coach, who was supposed to be developing the new talent already within the club, to overlook them so regularly. Nevertheless, my figures didn't compare favourably with most of the other apprentices from 1969 intake.

Only Peter Whitwood, who had left the club, had played less games than me. Paul McEwan, who signed part-way through the season had played 12 matches, with the rest of the lads playing 30 or more times. The Schoolboy International pedigree of Ronny Goodlass, Mick Buckley and Ray Pritchard had developed and they had been drafted in to form part of Tommy Casey's 'A' Team Squad during the second half of the season. Some of the older apprentices had continued their development with Peter Scott and Alan Wilson getting into double figures in appearances for the Reserves in the Central League with John Smith playing once. The remainder of the older apprentices were fielded in either the 'B' or 'A' Teams, but all played significantly more games than I had managed.

Put in this context, it was easy to see how Stewart viewed my prospects. The statistics may have made a compelling case in his eyes for me to go in order to make room for signing a new schoolboy centre forward to take my place in the close season. I knew that was Stewart's prerogative. His job and his own future prospects as a coach at Everton depended on being successful with his team. He had players in his squad who had progressed and remained free of injury and he had to make decisions that ensured that only the best players were retained. This realisation and the memory of my run-ins with Stewart over my first injury and little issues like his failure to supply me with new boots when I needed them resulted in me having no doubts about what my future prospects at Everton were in his eyes.

The situation I found myself in meant that I needed some guidance and advice about what to do. Stewart had made it clear what his position was and I felt that I couldn't 'go over his head' to speak to any of the other coaching staff or Chief Scout Harry Cook for fear of making the situation worse. Other apprentices or the pros were too busy concentrating on their own careers to have time to get involved with fighting anyone else's corner.

In any case, it was accepted that someone leaving the club was sometimes secretly interpreted as a positive for some players who remained, as it meant one less competitor for a shirt in their position on a Saturday afternoon. We had learned very quickly that football was a ruthless and cut-throat business and that, by necessity, people looked after themselves first.

I soon worked out that my only recourse was to have a long conversation with my dad about what my options were and then to see my old PE Teacher,

Bob Downing, who had always been a source of good advice in the past.

Both my dad and Bob were very supportive when we discussed what choices I had; the option of being released to another club to continue my apprenticeship in a fresh start (maybe Burnley might still be interested); leaving by mutual consent with the club paying up my contract, resigning and going to college full-time to further my qualifications; staying put and seeing out my contract.

In the end after hours of mulling things over in my own mind, I resolved to see out my contract on the basis that my second season could not be as much of a nightmare as my first was at times. I was determined not to be forced out and to make the most of what remained of my opportunity at Everton. I was still determined to show what I was capable of and to prove to Stewart that I was a better player than he was giving me credit for.

MAY 1970
OUT WITH THE OLD

The contrast between the constant activity and pace of life at Bellefield during the season and the quiet, almost sedate atmosphere during the close season was palpable. Everton's England World Cup Squad members had left to meet up with Alf Ramsey as they prepared for their defence of the Jules Rimet Trophy in Mexico. The rest of the first-team squad and full-time pros continued with their scaled-down training regimes as they wound down from a frenetic season and awaited the start of their summer vacations. Good humour abounded as everyone at the club reflected on a highly successful season at all levels.

The First Division Title was clearly the jewel in the crown but the club as a whole enjoyed some pleasing results. Stewart Imlach's 'B' Team had proved a force to be reckoned with in the Lancashire League, as had the 'A' Team coached by Tommy Casey. Only the Reserves had something of a mixed season and although finishing respectably high up in the Central League, they were ultimately comfortably eclipsed by winners Liverpool Reserves.

Groundsman Sid McGuinness, as usual, kept us up to date as speculation began to circulate at the training ground about potential signings for the first-team and who might be transferred out of the club. A rumour also began doing the rounds as to whether Arthur Proudler, the Reserve Team coach would remain at the club for the following season. This in turn fuelled rumours regarding who Arthur's successor might be if indeed he was to leave Everton. As it happened, the rumours proved to be right but we were still shocked when we turned up one morning and before training, Stewart Imlach and Tommy Casey confirmed to us that Arthur had in fact left the club and wouldn't be seen at Bellefield again.

There was no mention of who Arthur's replacement as Reserve Team coach would be resulting further speculation, not only as to who the new coach would be, but also the reasons for him leaving. It was merely conjecture, but in the apprentices dressing room, various theories were mooted; a fall out with Wilf Dixon or Harry Catterick; a disagreement about wages; criticism of his coaching style; or simply finishing below Liverpool who had won the Central League for the second year running.

It did seem strange that Arthur left without the opportunity for us to say our goodbyes to him. I always found him a knowledgeable and approachable coach, who seemed to get closer to his players and use a lot more humour and psychology than Stewart or Tommy ever did. I was always grateful to him for making me and the other Kirkby lads who went to our first training sessions as schoolboys at Bellefield feel so welcome. But this was professional football – and if it wasn't already clear, the cruel and unsentimental side of the game was soon to be demonstrated to us.

****

If speculation about the coaching staff and who Everton might be signing in the close season was rife, it was nothing when compared to the intense discussions amongst the youngsters on the playing staff, surrounding which of the older apprentices would be signed on as full-time pros and who would be released. The situation with apprentices and signing a full professional contract had been explained to all of us when we signed our apprenticeship contracts before leaving school. We all knew that at some stage before our eighteenth birthdays, the club had to make its mind up; or rather the coaching staff had to make their recommendations to the manager about who they thought should be signed as a full-time pro, and who should be let go.

Now that the season was over, our training had been scaled down and more of our time was once again dedicated to the mundane close season tasks involved in grounds maintenance. Tasks like wheelbarrowing soil around the pitches, painting goal posts and all manner of other labour intensive duties aimed at preparing Bellefield for the start of pre-season training when everyone returned from their summer holidays.

During this tedious work, we had little else to talk about other than which of us apprentices would be signed and who would be leaving. We knew that any of the older apprentices could be called up into manager Harry Catterick's office at any time to discover what their fate was to be. Joe Moran, Les Ormrod, Peter Scott, Alan Wilson and John Smith were approaching their eighteenth birthdays and, therefore, the end of their apprentice contracts and a sense of intense anticipation surrounded them as they tried to go about their duties without worrying about being summoned to the manager's office. As each day went by without any word from the manager, the tension in the apprentice's dressing room mounted until finally, first Les and then Joe were called in quick succession to Harry Catterick's office one lunchtime.

Both cut reluctant figures as they made the long walk upstairs to a waiting Harry Catterick as the rest of us waited expectantly in the dressing room to hear the outcome of their interviews with the Boss. After what seemed an eternity, it was clear when they returned that it was bad news for both of them.

Les came back first, walking slowly and silently to his place before sitting down and calmly announcing that he would be leaving and that he would be joining Stockport County on trial. With that he climbed out of his training gear, showered and dressed before shaking everyone's hand, saying his goodbyes without the slightest emotion and leaving with his boots tucked under his arm.

Joe's reaction was different. We could hear his emotional sobbing before he reached the dressing room. He was totally inconsolable as he slammed the door and collapsed in a wretched heap on the floor. His best mates from their Liverpool Boys days, John Smith and Alan Wilson were nearly as distraught as Joe as they tried to comfort him and sympathise with him. Their best buddy and team-mate was leaving and there was nothing he or they could do about it.

We were all stunned by how shattered Joe had been by the news and it was difficult not to feel compassion and sympathy for him as he tried in vain to come to terms with the fact that within hours he would no longer be a player at the club he so obviously loved.

Unlike Les, Joe's farewells were long and tearful and he virtually had to be escorted from the training ground such was his reluctance to leave Bellefield for the last time. We were sad to see him go. Always a hard worker and trainer, Joe was a skilful defender-cum-midfielder who loved it at Everton and was a fund of jokes and anecdotes that kept everyone in good spirits. But both he and Les had failed to reach the standard required to be one of the two or three apprentices each year who were recommended by the coaching staff to be offered a full professional contract. This brutal truth had been graphically illustrated to us in the space of a few minutes.

Later on, I was struck by the contrast between Les and Joe when they received their bad news and how they dealt with the rejection and how prepared they had been for that particular eventuality. On one hand Les had presumably envisaged the possibility of being released and had accepted that there was an alternative for him by agreeing to join Stockport County, which made sense because it was a lower League side near his home town of Manchester, where he could continue in the game and attempt to resurrect his career. Joe, meanwhile, seemed to have given little thought to the consequences of not being offered a full professional contract and what he would do next, which resulted in such a devastated reaction from him.

It proved a salutary lesson for us all.

It was a lesson I personally took on board. It was coming up to the time I was due to sit my 'O' Level exams at Childwall Hall. Seeing first hand with Les and Joe how things might turn out encouraged me to try that little bit harder with my preparation and revision.

****

The end of the season and the approaching summer break for the players didn't discourage the usual gaggle of Everton fans from congregating at the gates of the training complex in the hope of catching a glimpse of their heroes as they came and went from Bellefield. To be fair, most of the first-team players stopped to sign at least one or two of the autograph books, which were thrust hopefully towards their car windows as they were passing by the fans as they waited patiently at the entrance.

After training one morning and having lunch in the canteen, the apprentices were ordered to make our way down to Goodison to help with sorting out match kit from the laundry and to take care of running repairs on the match boots for the first-team. As luck would have it, as we dispersed to catch the bus along Queens Drive, Howard Kendall was leaving at the same time and stopped us on the car park and asked if anybody wanted a lift to Goodison as he was heading that way himself. So five of us squeezed into his pristine blue Jaguar and headed off towards the gates of the training ground with me sitting proudly in the front seat. As usual, the car was surrounded by waiting autograph hunters as it got to the exit and Howard stopped to sign a few prior to carrying on.

It was a warm day and both front windows of the car were already wound down to allow for some ventilation. The fans were handing in their books for Howard to sign from both sides of the car and to speed things up I was handing some to him from the front passenger side window for him to sign and then returning them to their owners. This didn't prevent a bit of a traffic jam forming behind us and a few impatient beeps from the queue of players' cars waiting to leave Bellefield at the same time as us. So Howard cut short his autographing session in order to clear the gates and he soon had us delivered to Goodison to start our afternoon's work, after which we made our way home.

This was a typically uneventful, run of the mill, ordinary afternoon. That was a view that changed dramatically when I arrived at Bellefield the following morning.

After getting into our training gear, the apprentices were sat around in casual conversation, when without warning the changing room door burst open and we were met by young pros Steve Seargeant and Alec Clarke from the dressing room next door pointing at me and shouting,"You! Next door now! Court Case!!!!"

And with that, before I could react, I was man-handled by the two of them out of the room and into the pros dressing room where I was met by a wall of stony faced inquisitors who sat, arms folded in silent judgement as I was sat down and held on a chair beneath the large mirror that was fixed to the wall at one end of the changing room.

Colin Harvey and Howard Kendall sign autographs at Bellefield

"What the f**k's all this about!" I shouted indignantly.

Without responding, Alec Clarke assumed the role of chief inquisitor.

"It has come to the attention of this court that yesterday afternoon, you were seen signing autographs for the fans at the entrance to Bellefield whilst a passenger in Howard Kendall's car. It is the opinion of this court that you are guilty of blatantly being 'Big Time' and acting above your station as an apprentice. Have you anything to say in your defence?"

Alec's mock-legal tone amused the rest of the pros, who sat expectantly waiting for my reply. I was panicking, thinking back to Peter Whitwood and his distraught reaction to being the subject of a 'court case'. I was also angry at the injustice of the 'charge' I was facing.

"I didn't sign any friggin' autographs. You can ask Howard or any of the lads in the car with me. I only handed the books to Howard to sign and gave them back!" I protested.

Ignoring my plea, Alec continued, "No need for witnesses, we have witnesses of our own who were in the car behind you and saw what was happening. Why should we believe the apprentices?"

He then addressed the room saying, "All those who find the defendant guilty, say 'Aye'." A resounding, 'Aye' rang out and attention returned to Alec who, in his role as 'judge', was donning a pair of black shorts on his head, by way of an improvised judge's black cap for sentencing. In an austere voice and holding a size 12 Dunlop Green Flash, Alec announced, "I hereby sentence the accused to six strokes of the pump to be administered immediately!"

My heart sank as Alec moved forward brandishing the pump menacingly and I felt the grip on my shoulders as some of the other pros started to restrain me in case I fled from my punishment.

Flushed with anger and adrenalin, I shot out of my seat and grabbed the nearest thing to me that I could use to defend myself. It happened to be a large white metal enamel jug, which was usually filled with tea or squash for refreshment at the end of each training session. As Alec approached me I swung the jug round in an enormous arc aiming at his head. As I did so he ducked out of the way just in time and my momentum swung me around crashing the jug into the mirror, which shattered loudly into a thousand pieces and fell along with the jug noisily to the floor causing my accusers to recoil momentarily away from me.

I used the moment of confusion to make my escape. Crunching across the broken glass, I grabbed the door handle and flung open the door and sped down the corridor in the direction of the first-team dressing room with Alec, still wearing his judge's 'black cap', in hot pursuit. The noise of the shattering mirror must have been heard throughout the building because as I tore around the corner of the corridor towards the first-team dressing room I ran headlong into a half changed Johnny Morrissey who had emerged to investigate what had happened.

Johnny Morrissey was short in stature but was built like a pocket-sized Hercules, all bulging calf muscles, rippling thighs and six-pack stomach. I felt as if I'd run into a brick wall and bounced off him landing on my back on the corridor floor winded and gasping for air. Alec screeched to a halt behind me and we both looked at Johnny waiting for his reaction. In the few seconds it took me to regain my senses after hitting the floor, he had worked out exactly what was going on and why Alec was pursuing me.

"Leave him alone and f**k off Clarkey", said Morrissey staring right into Alec's eyes with a look of a Liverpool nightclub bouncer. Alec didn't need telling twice and turned on his heel and slunk off in the direction of his own dressing room. As one or two of the other first-team players emerged into the corridor, Johnny was kind enough to help me up and ask me if I was OK and what the sound of glass breaking was. I explained that I had shattered the mirror whilst protecting myself with the enamel jug.

Johnny laughed and said, "That's just what I'd have done too if they tried to give me that shit. Don't worry lad, after that they won't be bothering you again".

Johnny Morrissey was right, they didn't!

JUNE 1970
WORLD CUP
FEVER

During the first two weeks of June, the whole of the country was transfixed with events that were beamed via satellite into our living rooms from Mexico as the England Football Team began its defence of the World Cup. Conversation at Bellefield was of little else as the build-up to each of their matches intensified, particularly as Everton players Brian Labone, Alan Ball, Tommy Wright and Keith Newton were likely to play key roles as the tournament unfolded.

In gruelling heat and at high altitude England were scheduled to play their three group stage matches within the space of ten days. A 1-0 win over Romania provided the positive start that everyone was hoping for, which meant the stand-out group stage match against favourites Brazil was next up for England. In searing temperatures England put in an impressive display but eventually went down 1-0 in spite of world class displays from captain Bobby Moore and goalkeeper Gordon Banks. However, England put that disappointment behind them and secured qualification to the quarter-finals with a 1-0 victory in their final group match against Czechoslovakia.

England's qualification as runners-up in their group to Pele's Brazil set up a tantalising tie in the last eight against losing finalists from 1966, West Germany. The nation was riveted as the eagerly awaited clash against the Germans approached when England were dealt a serious blow before the quarter final, as it emerged that Gordon Banks had been struck down by a mysterious illness and was ruled out of the match. Understudy Peter Bonnetti, the Chelsea goalkeeper was selected to play in goal as the nation crowded around its TV sets watching expectantly.

Words couldn't really describe the disappointment felt throughout the country as England surrendered a two goal lead and it was the West Germans who prevailed 3-2 in a thrilling encounter to qualify for the semi-finals and leave England to return home early from the tournament when they looked to have a place in the last four wrapped up.

'Back Home' everyone at Everton took some consolation from the contribution made by the Everton players with Alan Ball playing in all four of England's matches and Keith Newton and Brian Labone in three each with

Tommy Wright appearing in two games. But when the dust had settled, the one question that remained unanswered, especially amongst Everton fans, was whether England would have surrendered a two goal lead against West Germany if Gordon West had been understudy to Gordon Banks instead of Peter Bonnetti? It was a question that was to be debated long after the World Cup was over.

* * * *

By the time England had made their unexpected exit from the World Cup, decisions on coaching and apprentice personnel at Everton had already been made in readiness for the start of the 1970/1971 season.

We learned that as a result of Arthur Proudler leaving the club, Tommy Casey had been promoted to Reserve Team coach and that Stewart Imlach had been elevated to the 'A' Team. This was seen as reward for them both for the excellent results they had achieved in the Lancashire league in the previous season. Whilst it was obviously good news for Tommy and Stewart, from a selfish point of view, I couldn't help feeling a twinge of disappointment that Stewart would continue as a coach of the youngsters at the club and that this would obviously have a bearing on my own prospects because of the less than ideal relationship I had had with him during my first season at Everton.

The one glimmer of hope for me personally was that a new coach had been appointed to the club to be in charge of the 'B' Team. Tommy and Stewart called a meeting of the apprentices to inform us that the new coach was going to be Ian Crawford, the ex-Hearts, West Ham and Peterborough winger who would be joining the club for the start of pre-season training. Whilst I hadn't heard of Ian's name before, it at least gave me cause for optimism that I would be able to make a fresh start with a new coach and hopefully put the trials and tribulations of my first season behind me and start to make up some of the ground I felt I'd lost on the other apprentices.

Three apprentices who would be following Stewart and Tommy up the pecking order at Everton and into the ranks of the full time professionals were Peter Scott, Alan Wilson and John Smith. The day they were called for their interviews with the manager was in direct contrast to the one we witnessed for Les Ormrod and Joe Moran a few weeks earlier. Each of them returned grinning from ear-to-ear having been offered full professional contracts by Harry Catterick, which they had no hesitation in signing there and then. Within days they had vacated their places with us in the apprentice's dressing room, having earned their right of passage next door into the professional's dressing room amid a huge amount of mickey taking from the older more established players.

Nobody begrudged Peter, Alan and John their success. They were all outstanding young players. Peter was a strong tackling right back and had

Twice behind in last week's game against Arsenal, we gained an important point thanks to two goals from Alan Whittle. In the top picture, Alan (right) fires home following a right-wing corner and, below, beats Bob Wilson with a shot through a packed goalmouth.

made several appearances in the Reserves and trained regularly with Arthur Proudler and his squad the previous season. Similarly Alan Wilson had also made the breakthrough into the Central League squad as an up-and-coming, powerfully built centre forward with a good eye for goal. John or 'Tigsy', as he was more often called, more than made up for his slight stature with a tigerish approach to playing in midfield, had also made his first appearance for the Reserves.

It occurred to me that all three of them had managed to remain on a path of development that provided their careers as apprentices with a trajectory that resulted in them securing a professional contract. That trajectory consisted of a first season playing predominantly for the 'B' Team but making a breakthrough into the 'A' Team squad. Their second season was predominantly playing for the 'A' Team and their final apprentice season making the breakthrough into the Reserves. This was a steep curve of progression and required ability, application, determination and more than a slice of good fortune in avoiding serious injuries. It was a career development path that we all aspired to. Unfortunately for me, on reflection, I realised how far behind my own career path had slipped and how hard I was going to have to work if I was to get it back on track.

As far as Peter, Alan and John were concerned, though, they were enjoying their new-found status as full-time pros and wasted no time in coming back into the apprentices dressing room and jokingly demanding fresh training gear or complaining that their boots were not clean enough. John also wasted no time in deciding what to invest his signing-on fee in and arrived one morning, the proud owner of a brand new Ford Cortina Mark 2 1200cc saloon. It was a basic model with light blue paintwork and a plastic and PVC interior and upholstery but 'Tigsy' was obviously very proud of his newly acquired wheels as he invited us to have a look around it. Whilst it was no World Cup Squad Cortina 1600E, the symbolism of the new car for the new fully fledged professional footballer was not lost on us apprentices.

With Les and Joe being released and Peter, Alan and John signing their full professional contracts, there was obviously room for a fresh batch of new apprentices to be introduced to the club and it wasn't long before rumours began to circulate about who the latest recruits would be.

Two players who had been making a name for themselves amongst the schoolboy ranks on Merseyside and attracting the attention of club scouts were Kirkby Boys captain and midfield player, Jimmy Burns and a free-scoring centre forward with Huyton Boys by the name of George Telfer. We'd heard quite a bit about the two of them because most of us were still in touch with our respective coaches from our schoolboy days; and there was always good coverage in the local press of the schools' football scene. If Everton's scouting network was doing its usual job of sifting through the local talent, it was confidently predicted that these two high-profile schoolboys would soon be coming on board.

* * * *

With the Mexico World Cup over and most of the basic grounds work at Bellefield completed ready for the commencement of pre-season training in July, we were grateful to be told that we were officially on holiday for two weeks. The training ground was already a quiet and eerie place as all of the full-time pros had already started their holidays the week before. We were happy to leave Dougie Rose and Sid McGuinness to their own devices in the groundsman's hut as we left Bellefield with a spring in our steps, eager to discover what two weeks of freedom from our arduous training routine would be like.

One or two of the apprentices went off immediately to holidays at resorts around the coast in England or Wales. Some were even lucky enough to fly off with their families for a package holiday to Spain! I wasn't so lucky as financially, a holiday was still out of reach for me. The same was true of the other Kirkby lads at Everton, Ray Pritchard and Paul McEwan, so we contented ourselves, along with our mates, to the odd day out at Southport or Formby instead.

We also discovered the pleasure of golf. A municipal golf course had been opened on Valley Road on the outskirts of Kirkby and naturally we were interested in learning how to play the game. We often heard the pros, particularly the first-team, discussing their keen involvement in playing at their respective golf clubs in the leafy suburbs around Liverpool. As aspiring professional footballers, we loftily imagined making the grade as players at Everton and having the luxury of afternoons off training to relax and recouperate on the golf course instead of mopping floors and cleaning boots.

The reality, of course, was very different.

Our first foray into the noble game of golf was taking turns with a rusty 6 iron on the playing fields of Brookfield school. In spite of the club having a slightly bent shaft, we managed to get the rudiments of a swing sorted out using golf balls that we 'acquired' from the Pitch and Putt facility next to Kirkby Golf Course. Having managed to beg, steal or borrow a hotch-potch of other clubs and putters, we progressed quickly onto the Pitch and Putt course, playing mainly at dusk, sneaking through a hole in the perimeter fence after the course had closed.

Very soon, although still at the 'hacking' stage in the development our emerging golf swings, we ventured onto the main 18 hole municipal golf course. This presented a whole new set of challenges to us as fledgling golfers before we even got onto the course, such as each borrowing a set of golf clubs or, as a last resort, hiring a half-set to play with. Once out on the golf course, we were not intimately familiar with the intricacies of the Royal and Ancient Rules of Golf and had to suffice with our own local rules or 'Kirkby Rules' as we knew them. For example, missing the ball completely with an 'air shot' didn't count, but breaking wind anywhere on the course whilst an opponent was playing his shot did count as a 'foul-air shot'; and placing and teeing the ball up in the rough was allowed in order to 'give it a good twatting'.

Inevitably the competitive spirit amongst us emerged and we couldn't play without a series of rewards and forfeits being introduced to our 'Kirkby Rules'. Examples of this were, having to pay 10p to your opponents if your putt was so bad that it rolled off the green; playing the next hole with your trouser legs rolled up if you scored a 10 or worse; and most embarrassingly, playing the hole with your penis hanging out of your trousers if your tee shot failed to go further than the ladies tee!

It was good knock about fun and in fact we all made a decent fist of the basics of the game, especially Paul McEwan who showed a natural aptitude for golf, so much so that a few months afterwards he was playing regularly enough and well enough to be given his first ever handicap of 16 at Kirkby Municipal Golf Club!

But as June came to an end, our thoughts and discussions on the golf course turned inevitably to returning to Bellefield and the start of pre-season training for the 1970/71 season. We all had our views about what challenges lay ahead as we re-joined the other apprentices and the race to make the grade as a pro at Everton.

JULY 1970
A SLICE OF
HUMMEL PIE

When the players returned to Bellefield from their summer jaunts, it was easy to see which of them had been abroad to sunnier climes. Suntans of various shades were on prominent display as the bright summer clothes were exchanged for drab training gear and the hard grind of pre-season training got under way again. It was obvious immediately that the methods that served the club so well during Everton's championship winning campaign were not going to be abandoned as the forced marches around the training ground began in earnest as the precursor to a month of gruelling fitness, stamina and conditioning work. One interesting change to our preparation for the coming season resulted from the club qualifying for the European Cup as English Champions. One morning the whole of the playing staff had to report in batches to the Physio's Room where Norman Borrowdale assisted the club doctor in administering a series of injections and inoculations intended to protect us against tetanus, malaria and all manner of hazards we might encounter whilst abroad.

The mood around the training ground was positive and upbeat as we all settled down into our routines with our respective coaches. Ian Crawford, the new 'B' Team coach had been introduced to everyone at the customary pre-season meeting of the playing staff and coaches and we were gradually getting to know him and his methods as the days elapsed.

With no signings amongst the full professional ranks for the club during the close season, personnel and the organisation of our apprentices kit and boot duties remained largely unchanged with the exception of Jimmy Burns and George Telfer filling in some of the gaps left by Peter Scott, Alan Wilson et al having duly arrived as new fresh-faced apprentices as predicted.

The dressing rooms were awash with tales of 'daring do' and the romantic adventures from the holidays the players had enjoyed in exotic far-off places, which contrasted vividly with my own summer sorties to Formby sands and Kirkby Golf Course.

By far the most captivating of the tales regaled to rapt audiences, including us apprentices, between training sessions were those provided by

Everton's returning World Cup quartet fresh from the tournament in Mexico. Looking lean and bronzed, Alan Ball, Brian Labone, Keith Newton and Tommy Wright held court with their stories of life with Alf Ramsey's England during the World Cup. They described what it was like to play in temperatures of over 100 degrees Fahrenheit and to lose up to eight pounds in weight through fluid loss during 90 minutes of football.

Everyone was eager to know more about the furore surrounding the arrest of Bobby Moore prior to the World Cup when the England team were in Columbia on a warm up tour prior to the Mexico Tournament. Alan Ball explained that the first they knew about the arrest was when Bobby Charlton and Bobby Moore returned to the team hotel to explain to Alf Ramsey that Moore had been detained by the police to make a statement about an alleged theft after they had left a jewellery shop they had been into looking for a present for Charlton's wife. A week later, having denied the allegation, Moore was placed under house arrest at the home of a local football official. He was freed three days later to continue on to Mexico to captain the England team. Bally described the incredible pressure Moore must have been under as the world's media held siege to the England hotel and how dignified he remained throughout his ordeal. The general feeling in the England camp was, according to Ball, that the accusations levelled at Bobby Moore were a publicity stunt aimed at disrupting England's preparations for the World Cup and to undermine team morale, rather than the sinister blackmail plot by Columbian gangsters, which was dreamt up and suggested in some sections of the media.

Asked about England's 3-2 defeat to West Germany in the quarter-final and the suggestion by some commentators that the substitution of Bobby Charlton and the subsequent influence on the game of Franz Beckenbauer was crucial, Brian Labone was adamant that it was impossible to tell whether it was a defining factor especially as Beckenbauer had scored while Charlton was still on the pitch.

All four players maintained a neutral stance when the question of Peter Bonetti's goalkeeping performance as Gordon Banks' replacement in the West Germany game was raised. Asked directly if he thought England would have won against the Germans if Gordon West had played instead of Bonetti, they shrugged their shoulders and Alan Ball added, "Very possibly, but we'll never know, will we?"

Gordon West maintained a very diplomatic silence.

It was a surreal experience for us youngsters listening in on these conversations as we went about our duties. Matches and international news items that had been televised worldwide and become the topic of fierce debate were being discussed in front of us a few short weeks later by players who had been directly involved.

****

One piece of news that was high up the local news agenda was the announcement in the press that Alan Ball had signed a boot sponsorship deal with German boot manufacturer Hummel. He'd let it be known at Bellefield that Hummel had offered him a deal worth £2,000 to wear their distinctive white boots. The deal meant that he had to dispense with his old Adidas boots for both training and matches. As a result of this Ball needed several pairs of boots broken in quickly to avoid the risk of blisters. It was normal practice for some of the first-team players to give apprentices their new boots to wear for a couple weeks to break them in and soften the leather and there was no shortage of volunteers to do this for them.

Hence a few days after Alan Ball had done the deal with Hummel, he appeared unannounced at the apprentice's dressing room door carrying an arm full of brand new Hummel boots. He simply threw the boots into the middle of the room and shouted, "If you wear size seven's, break these in for me, I want them back at the end of next week!" He then left us to it.

After a moment's stunned silence, all hell broke loose as the assembled apprentices fought for a pair of those special boots. Ronny Goodlass was first away into the showers with the first pair, Mick Buckley slid a pair under the bench and jammed them there with his feet and John Smith, who happened to be in there from the pros dressing room, lay on top of a pair grasping them like a limpet.

That left one pair. And it was me or Davey Graham in a fight to the death to see who got them. We pulled, we pushed. We gritted our teeth. We grunted and snarled. This was getting serious.

"Come on lads, that's enough", someone said. We didn't hear him as elbows started to fly, heads butted, oaths were uttered and blood and snot flew.

Then out of the blue, my grip on the boots slipped and I lurched backwards. The rest was a blur. I was told later that my head bounced off the changing room wall, but all I could remember was coming to and seeing Davey's smirk as he tried on the white Hummel boots – the white Hummel boots that should have been mine! I wasn't about to forget that.

The incident was soon forgotten by everyone (except me) as the arduous grind of pre-season training got into full swing and after a few days, I was pleased to see that Davey had got blisters from the Hummel boots. Then the dreaded announcement was made that we would be making our annual trip to Ainsdale.

The day arrived just as it had done the year before and the same exhausting and torturous ritual was repeated as we scaled new heights across and up and down the mountainous sand hills on the Lancashire coast. Then, finally, deliverance. It was football on the beach and an added bonus of a five-a-side tournament. When everyone had been organised by the coaching staff, I ended up playing in a match being refereed by Stewart Imlach. Davey Graham was on the opposing team and I couldn't help noticing that he was wearing Alan Ball's white Hummel boots.

Quite a crowd had gathered on the beach as word had got around that Everton FC were training there. But I wasn't really interested in spectators, I was more interested in getting revenge on Davey. It wasn't long before the opportunity I was waiting for arrived. My team was awarded a direct free kick and I grabbed the ball and placed it carefully on the sand about 15 yards from goal.

"Make a wall, two men, right hand post!" the goalie shouted.

Davey duly obliged as I was taking aim – not at the goal, but at Davy's goolies! My run up was short but my shot was hard and straight......and accurate! Bingo! Right on the button, Davey went down like a sack of pro-verbial. To his credit though, he was up in a second and after me. We then proceeded to knock seven shades out of one another until we were restrained and separated. And all of this overseen and witnessed by the first-team, Reserves, coaching staff and the general public amid lots of questions and enquiries about what had provoked us.

Back at Bellefield, with me sporting a shiner and Davey with a split lip, we were ordered into the indoor training area by Stewart. He subjected us to half an hour of sprint shuttle runs until we were sick as punishment for a 'breach of club discipline'. After we had dragged ourselves wearily away, showered and dressed, we settled our differences as we caught the bus together long after the others had gone.

Over the following couple of days, as normal training resumed, we both got loads of stick including being called 'Cassius' or 'Our Enery'; or Johnny Morrissey cowering in the corner in mock terror as either of us walked past. As expected, Alan Ball returned to the apprentice's dressing room and reluc-tantly the four test dummies had to hand back their prized Hummel boots, suitably softened and supple after being broken in. As he disappeared from the room I thought my chance of ever wearing his white boots had gone with him. I was wrong.

Batch No.2 of white boots arrived a few days later. As before, Alan Ball sought suitable size 7's from amongst the apprentices. But this time he didn't throw the boots into the room causing minor mayhem. Instead he approached four lads and gave them the boots once he had confirmed their boot size. I was the first one he asked and gratefully grabbed them before he had the chance to change his mind. I would like to say that for the next two weeks, the boots made me play like Alan Ball, but unfortunately the similar-ity ended with the colour of the boots and the colour of our ginger locks.

Sadly and all too soon the time came to hand the boots back. I made a special point of cleaning the boots really thoroughly. I even got some 'Vim' scouring powder from the cleaning cupboard so they were extra white when I went to the first-team dressing room to hand them over after training. There were only a couple of players left when I knocked the door and went in.

"I've brought your boots back Alan", I said grudgingly.

"Thanks, just drop them down there", he said glancing up from his newspaper.

"You had a lovely shiner the other week didn't you? Did you get that at Ainsdale?" he continued.

"Yeah, me and Davey Graham had a scrap and.......", I explained, but he interrupted me.

"Yeah, I know all about it", he said.

I just shrugged my shoulders and turned to leave when he pointed to the white boots beside him and said, "On second thoughts, you might as well keep hold of those".

He picked the boots up and threw them to me and I caught them as I stood there speechless. As I stepped towards the door, he winked and said, "No need to get into any more scraps now, eh?"

I just smiled, looked at the boots and said, "No, not now I've got these".

I treasured those boots, not because they were white or because they were new and novel, but because of who gave them to me. It was an act of kindness the memory of which would stay with me for many years.

****

As a footnote to this episode, sadly for Hummel boots and Alan Ball, as the season wore on, it became clear that their partnership was never going to be a marriage made in heaven. Putting it bluntly he just didn't get on with the new boots. He frequently complained that the leather was not as good in quality as he was used to in the 'Adidas 2000' boots that he and most of the other first-team players at Everton played in. At one stage he even asked us to 'whiten' a pair of his Adidas boots for one match, leaving the black gap between the three stripes to look like to two chevron-shaped black stripes on the white Hummel boots – at least from a distance.

This was never going to work and the disguise came to grief when it rained during the match and the 'white' boots gradually turned black again. When this was noticed by the Hummel representatives, it signalled the beginning of the end for Alan Ball's sponsorship deal. However, in spite of reverting back to wearing Adidas, Alan Ball sporting his white Hummel boots for Everton remained an iconic image for us apprentices and I suspect for many Evertonians too.

****

For me, having Ian Crawford as our new coach was like a breath of fresh air. My relationship with Stewart Imlach during my first season at Everton couldn't really have been much worse but I seemed to hit it off with Ian almost immediately.

In his late 30's, Ian was a dapper man with a dark mop of tightly curled hair and a tanned, almost Mediterranean complexion. His effervescent enthusiasm about all of our training seemed to rub off on his squad as he took time to speak to each of us individually and explain about his goals and objectives for us and what he hoped to achieve in each session. Apart from our fitness and conditioning work, he worked methodically improving the full range of techniques and skills we would need to progress as players, utilising some innovative and imaginative drills and practices, which we had not experienced when being coached by Stewart or Tommy Casey. He even inspected all of our match boots, issuing new boots to replace any that weren't in pristine condition. He announced, "I can't ask you do the job without the right tools!" This was a refreshing change to having to go cap in hand to Stewart or Tommy when we thought we needed new boots.

I threw myself wholeheartedly into everything Ian arranged for us in the knowledge that nothing other than my total dedication and application was going to result in me standing a chance of securing a full professional contract during the remainder of my apprenticeship.

I admired Ian's honesty when he stated in a quite matter-of-fact way that he needed us to be successful as apprentices, because if we were successful it would mean he was achieving success and would be able to make progress in his career as a coach.

His more individualistic approach to coaching was put to good use when new apprentices Jimmy Burns and George Telfer arrived as Everton's newest recruits from Kirkby Boys and Huyton Boys respectively. Shy and withdrawn, Jimmy and George were assigned to myself and some of the other older apprentices to be shown the ropes and the duties they would be expected to perform ensuring a far less traumatic first few days than we had experienced a year earlier.

As I was showing them around the kit room and the Players' Lounge, it did occur to me how little time I had left at Everton to prove myself – only a year after starting my apprenticeship, I was showing the latest batch of promising talent around Bellefield, whilst arguably already having been assigned to the scrapheap at least in some people's eyes. This realisation served as an incredibly powerful motivation to redouble my efforts in all of Ian's training sessions and make the most of the time I had left on my contract in the hope securing another - as a full-time pro.

So as July drew to a close and the anticipation of August and the start of the 1970-1971 season grew, everything in the Everton Football Club garden seemed to be rosy. For the apprentices, a talented new coach had been installed, but more importantly, the First Division championship trophy gleamed in the Goodison Park Trophy Room and the youthful first-team squad bristled with international talent eager to once more scale the heights of domestic football. They relished the prospect of embarking on a European Cup campaign that promised further glory on foreign soil. Goodison Park, having hosted matches during the 1966 World Cup and already a prestigious ground, was being developed with a towering three-tier Main Stand to maintain its position as one of the pre-eminent football stadiums in the country and their modern Bellefield training complex was the envy of the league.

Even the captaincy of the club had been seamlessly ceded from one Goodison icon to another as Brian Labone handed the first-team reins to Alan Ball. With Harry Catterick, assisted by the talented Wilf Dixon, at the height of his powers continuing at the helm and supported by a Board of Directors with seemingly limitless financial resources to invest in the club, it seemed inevitable that a dynasty of successful teams would continue to roll off the Everton production line ensuring further silverware would adorn the Goodison Park Trophy Cabinet for years to come.

What could possibly go wrong?

AUGUST 1970 FALSE DAWN

I n a break with tradition, on 8th August 1970, the Charity Shield was played at Stamford Bridge, home of FA Cup Winners Chelsea. It was normally the privilege of the League Champions to host the season's curtain raiser but Everton were unable to stage the match due to work on the completion of the new Main Stand at Goodison Park reaching a crucial phase.

The change of venue didn't seem to affect Everton, who carried on where they left off the previous season securing a 2-1 victory thanks to goals from Howard Kendall and that man Alan Whittle to add the Charity Shield to the League Championship trophy. It seemed that normal service had resumed for Harry Catterick and his young Everton side.

What wasn't expected was Everton's run of league results for the remainder of August. An expectant crowd of over 50,000 left Goodison Park disappointed after a 2-2 draw against Arsenal in Everton's opening league game of the season. Three days later Burnley surprisingly earned a point at Goodison in a 1-1 draw with a defeat at Elland Road against fierce rivals Leeds United coming on the following Saturday. Further disappointments were suffered as the Toffees only managed a 2-2 draw at Stamford Bridge against Chelsea and ended their August fixtures with a 1-0 home defeat against Manchester City.

This was hardly the flying start to the new campaign that Harry Catterick or the Everton faithful were looking forward to. After the opening five league fixtures of the season the Champions had secured only three points and had failed to win any of their matches, three of which had been at home, resulting in a lowly league placing for the Toffees after the opening month of the new season.

The atmosphere at Bellefield was a far cry from the euphoria of the end of the triumphant season the first-team had just enjoyed. It was a mystery to everyone at the club as we all searched for reasons for this very uncharacteristic start to the 1970-1971 campaign.

A number of theories were bandied about. Were the manager and the board complacent in not securing any additions to the first-team squad during the close season to bolster and strengthen the team? Had the players been over confident in assuming their places in the squad were assured after winning the title? Had the exertions of the Mexico World Cup had a detrimental effect on the Everton players who played such an important role in England's defence of the Jules Rimet Trophy?

Whatever the reasons, a rapid improvement was needed if Everton were to stand any chance of retaining their League Title.

* * * *

For me the new season couldn't come quick enough as I and the rest of the apprentices reached peak fitness after an exhausting and demanding pre-season under Ian Crawford and Stewart Imlach's supervision. This was especially true as the Lancashire League had thrown up the tantalising prospect of two Mini-Derbies against Liverpool 'A' and 'B' Teams away at Liverpool's Melwood training ground on the opening day of the season!

To say we were fired up was an understatement as these Mini-Derbies were just as fiercely contested as the full blown version. I was doubly determined to show Ian Crawford what I was capable of and underline my commitment to his team if I was selected. When the team-sheets went up on the noticeboard at Bellefield on the Friday before the game, I was delighted to see that I had got the nod to over new apprentice George Telfer to start in the number nine shirt for the 'B' Team and couldn't wait for the match the following day.

At Melwood lots of friends and family of both teams had turned up to watch, which served as an additional incentive for all concerned.

In the dressing room before the game, Ian Crawford's team talk was very simple.

He said, "They have got a very strong team out. Most of them have played for the 'A' Team and one of the lads at the back has played for the Reserves. Just keep your shape and do your jobs and you'll be fine".

He then went through each player individually reminding them of their positions and responsibilities.

When he got to me he said, "Stan you're playing centre forward so push up on the centre half all the time. Get on his shoulder and use your speed – he's good in the air but slow on the turn. Look for the through ball on the deck".

Team talk over, we made our way out of the dressing room and onto the pitch. There was tension in the air as we psyched ourselves up to put one over on our closest neighbours and rivals.

The game was soon under way and, as you would expect in a Derby match, the tackles and challenges were soon flying in. It was all hundred-mile-an-hour stuff but it settled down after about 15 minutes. We were gradually getting on top and following Ian's instructions I felt I had the edge in speed on the tall gangly centre half but was caught narrowly offside a couple of times when clear on goal. Then after about half an hour, I judged my run perfectly and latched onto a through ball leaving my marker in my wake and slid the ball past the advancing goalkeeper – 1-0 to the Blues!

I nearly burst with pride – and better was to come! Just before half time in an almost identical move, I made it 2-0 – this was dreamland!

Unfortunately, we lost a bit of concentration and Liverpool pulled two quick goals back to make the half time score 2-2. When the whistle for the interval sounded, we were walking off the pitch and the centre half who was marking me turned to me and said, "You were f**king lucky with them two goals. You won't get past me again you ginger haired prick!"

I just winked at him and said," Well you'll have to be a bit quicker than you were in the first half you lanky twat!"

Ian's half-time team talk was straightforward.

He explained, "Keep things the same. Play the through ball for Stan – he's got the beating of their centre half every time, they're dead slow at the back".

Within a few minutes of the re-start, it was 3-2 to us. Mick Buckley drove in a rebound from a corner – we were coasting and started to pull them to pieces. With about ten minutes left, the icing was on the cake when I skated past the centre half yet again to knock in my third goal and make it 4-2 to us. What a feeling! It was like Christmas, Birthday and New Year's Eve all rolled into one.

On the way back for the restart after my hat-trick goal, the Liverpool centre half continued the verbals.

"Try that again and you'll be sorry", he threatened.

So I did – but this time he'd had enough and he was waiting for me. As I went past him, he scythed both legs from under me and I went down eating turf. I'm afraid the red mists descended in front of my eyes and before I could think I planted a left hook on his chin that Henry Cooper would have been proud of and he went down like a block of flats. The referee didn't have to send me off – I saved him the trouble by walking towards the dressing rooms, saying to him over my shoulder,

"The name's Osborne and when he wakes up, tell soft lad there it's 4-2 to Everton!"

Sadly, being down to ten men let an otherwise outplayed Liverpool back into the match in the closing stages and the game ended in a 4-4 draw.

Back in the dressing room Ian was full of praise for his side's performance and the way everyone had played to his tactical plan. However, at the end of his debrief he didn't spare my blushes when he ripped into me for losing my temper and getting myself sent off. Quite rightly he gave me the rollicking of my life and lectured me about not being professional enough and forgetting my responsibility to the team and being the cause of us only drawing such an important match when we had it virtually won. Naively, I thought Ian was going to praise me for scoring a hat-trick but instead I was subjected to the most humbling and chastening dressing down I had ever received. As I spent the rest of the weekend reflecting on what Ian had said to me, I concluded that it wasn't an experience I ever wanted to repeat and hoped I hadn't burnt any bridges with my new coach.

At least I needn't have worried on that score as I found out on Monday morning when I returned to training at Bellefield. Using a superb piece of psychology, Ian sent for me before training and spent about 15 minutes going over Saturday's game and in particular the three goals I had scored and where I could have improved my game. I realised afterwards that he had used the post-match debrief to knock me down a peg or two and was now focusing on the positives in order to motivate me. I came away with a renewed determination to put his advice into practice.

As a result of my sending off, I was suspended for two weeks but as luck would have it, the 'B' Team had no fixtures during that time and so I didn't actually miss a game. The only other match for the 'B' Team in August was on the 29th when we entertained Blackpool at Bellefield when I partnered George Telfer up front in his first game as an apprentice in a 1-1 draw. It was clear to me even at that early stage that George was a highly talented and motivated young centre forward and that I was going have my work cut out to stay ahead of him in the pecking order amongst the junior ranks at Everton.

* * * *

As well as being arguably the most talented young centre forward of his generation in the whole of England, Joe Royle was never slow in seeing an opportunity. The apprentices got the opportunity to see his business acumen in operation first hand at the start of the 1970/1971 season. As a reward for our efforts during the previous season, we were all allocated a complimentary season ticket for the first-team and reserve team fixtures at Goodison Park. Obviously, as players we weren't able to use them because of our own playing commitments on Saturdays, but the season ticket was a gesture by the club to the players with the intention that family members or friends would be able to make use of them as the club's guests. However, as most of our parents and families followed our games and supported us whenever they could, they were unlikely to be able to use our complimentary season tickets.

At the same time, many of the first-team often complained that they were never allocated sufficient complimentary tickets for their matches and were always on the lookout for spare tickets to satisfy the numerous requests they received. Joe Royle soon worked out that if he offered the right money to the impecunious apprentices at Everton, he would have a ready supply of complimentary season tickets to supplement his match day allocation. Always a favourite amongst the youngsters at the club, he wasted no time in doing the rounds in the apprentice's dressing room snapping up complimentary season tickets from any of us who were willing to part with them. After a brief spell of persuasion and bargaining, along with a lot of apprentices, I was happy to part with mine in exchange for a generous cash payment from Joe, which supplemented our meagre wages. It was a good deal all round and it was a pleasure doing business with him.

****

Such were the demands and intensity of our pre-season training regime, I had all but forgotten that the results of the three 'O' Level exams I had taken at the end of the summer term at Childwall Hall College were due in August. It took me a couple of minutes to realise what the contents of the envelope were likely to be when my mum passed it to me when I got home from training one evening.

Seeing the 'Joint Matriculation Board' emblem on the back of the envelope alerted me to the nature of the correspondence and I eagerly opened it to reveal that I had passed all three exams with decent grades. Added to the one pass I had secured before leaving Brookfield, that meant four 'O' Levels in total with courses on two more due to begin in September. As I absorbed this good news, I reflected on the sound advice given to me by my Head Teacher, Mr. Bury, about continuing my studies once I had left school. Bearing in mind my first year at Everton, I was glad I had taken it.

SEPTEMBER 1970
LOOKING UP

If Everton were hoping to put the run of poor results in the opening month of the season behind them with resounding league victory to start September, a visit to Old Trafford and a match against Manchester United would probably not have been their first choice of fixture. It proved to be a fruitless journey along the East Lancs Road with United running out comfortable 2-0 winners.

However, this defeat proved to be something of a turning point as Harry Catterick's team ran up six successive wins during the rest of the month resulting in a steady climb away from the lower reaches of the First Division and progress on the European front.

A 2-1 away win at West Ham United secured Everton's first league victory of the season and was followed up with a 2-0 win at Goodison Park against Ipswich Town. As a result of their improved form, Everton approached their first-round first-leg European Cup tie against Iceland Champions Keflavic in confident mood. A crowd of 28,000 witnessed an entertaining 6-2 win for the Toffees inspired by an Alan Ball hat-trick and two goals from Joe Royle.

A 2-0 away victory against Blackpool and a 3-1 home win against Crystal Palace meant a run of four league wins in September saw Everton climb to a much more respectable position in the league and the resumption of some of the stylish play which had seen them secure the league title in April. Harry Catterick's team rounded the month off in style with a 3-0 away leg win in Iceland to eliminate Keflavic 9-2 on aggregate and qualify for the second round of the European Cup where they were drawn against West German Champions, Borussia Moenchengladbach.

Returning to winning ways for the first-team in September put the smiles back on everyone's faces and a spring back into everyone's step at Bellefield as a far more positive mood prevailed. Things at last appeared to be looking up for Everton in their pursuit of a second successive championship.

****

Things weren't looking up quite so much in September for Ian Crawford and his 'B' Team though. The month started with the 'B' Team's first defeat of the season, 5-3 away to Blackburn Rovers. Again I partnered George Telfer in the forward line. Although George scored his first goal in an Everton shirt in this match, we didn't really gel as a front pairing but Ian persevered with us in our next match, which ended in a 1-1 draw at home against Tranmere Rovers. We were, however, able to end the month on a positive note when we secured a 1-0 away win at Preston North End.

Whilst our results were inconsistent, I felt that Ian was trying to get George Telfer and I to play a certain way – alternating who took up the central striking role with the other moving out to the left-wing. It was something we practiced regularly in training matches but was obviously new to both of us and was going to take time to develop. Another reason for the inconsistency in our results was the fact that Ian seldom had the opportunity to pick a settled side. There was obviously quite a bit of movement between the sides resulting from injuries and suspensions with players moving up and down the ranks as required. As a result the 'B' Team never fielded the same team in successive matches with apprentices like Ronny Goodlass, Mick Buckley, Ray Pritchard and Ian Bacon often moving between the 'A' and 'B' Teams.

Nevertheless it was good to be playing regularly, I felt fit, was free of injury and sensed I was finally beginning to make progress and starting to realise some of the potential I had as a player encouraged and spurred on by Ian Crawford and his coaching and training.

* * * *

Back home in Kirkby life went on pretty much as normal away from heady rarefied atmosphere of Everton Football Club. But football was never far away from peoples thoughts, as was the music of the Merseybeat at its peak and the latest swinging 60's fashions.

However, it has to be said that if you grew up in Liverpool in the early 60's there were two issues that were guaranteed to cause a debate/argument/nark on the housing estates in and around the city. The issues in question were simply 'red or blue?' and 'mod or rocker?'

You were either a committed Blues supporting Evertonian or a fanatical Red Kopite. There were two camps, no quarter asked or given – we are great, you are shite, whether the discussion was about Catterick's Blues or Shankly's Reds, Goodison or Anfield, Bellefield or Melwood, the players, the kit, the team coach, the club badge; the list was endless.

Likewise, you were either a scooter-driving 'Mod' or a motorbike riding 'Rocker'. Similarly, being a 'Mod' was the only way to be if you were that way inclined towards scooters, while the 'Greasers' only had eyes for followers of their motorbike cult.

I have to say it was interesting to note, in Kirkby at least, how the followers of the different football clubs and motorcycling cults managed to combine their allegiances and how this manifested itself. For example, it was possible to spot the odd Lambretta-revving Mod's crash helmet with EFC etched neatly across it in blue Airfix Model paint as they cruised the mean streets of Southdene. Conversely, there was an aging Rocker from West Vale who was noted for riding his BSA 500 in his leather jacket with silver studs across the back spelling out the unlikely legend, 'Hells Angels – Anfield Chapter'!

Our family was definitely of the Evertonian/Mods persuasion. Or to be more accurate the family were Evertonians and myself and my brother Alan were Mods. Alan was a fully-fledged, Lambretta-owning, Parka, Ben Sherman/thin black tie, sunglasses-wearing, proper Mod. Being three years younger, I was more what you might call a 'Mod by Proxy' because I didn't have a licence or the financial wherewithal to purchase the Mod gear let alone a scooter.

Alan's Lambretta was a joy to behold. Gleaming grey metallic paint, white-wall tyres and massive chrome frame at the front weighed down, Christmas tree-like, with about twenty gleaming rear view mirrors. We had also Evertonian-ised it by recreating the Everton badge in blue paint and lacquer on either engine side panel and securing a long aerial to the front fender with a triangular Everton flag resplendent at the tip.

The scooter became something of a minor icon for local kids and especially Evertonian kids who could indulge their interest in scooters and Everton at the same time whenever we were tinkering with the be-chromed vehicle.

Alan would repay my enthusiastic polishing of the chrome by giving me rides around the block from Aldford Road – provided the police weren't about. Some of the local Evertonian kids were treated to a ride around the block as well, again provided the coast was clear. Liverpool supporting youngsters who requested a turn in the pillion seat were invariably told politely to, "Piss off until yer support a decent team!"

We would have to keep a very sharp look out for the blue and white police Ford Anglias and Escorts which regularly patrolled the area. Alan had been stopped quite a few times and warned about carrying passengers whilst still a learner driver so he was a known face to the law.

One of our neighbours and close mates, John Hough, was always keen to have a ride on the back of Alan's scooter. John was a tall, gangly, spotty youth of about sixteen with unusually long thin legs and thick mop of lank brown hair. He was also prone to wearing ridiculously wide flared trousers with turn-ups and boots with Cuban heels which made him look even taller.

One Saturday we had spent most of the morning fitting the latest Mod fashion accessory to Alan's scooter – a chrome luggage rack behind the rear seat and we were proudly showing it off to the usual gathering of admirers, including the gangly John Hough. John, dressed in his usual garb managed to persuade Alan to let him ride pillion. So as about a dozen of us looked on Alan revved up and set off at great speed out of Aldford Road, left into Cawthorn Avenue, which arced round into Rockford Avenue and left again into Aldford Road, coming to a halt outside number 21, a circuit of just over a quarter of a mile.

John was just about to dismount when Alan looked over his shoulder and shouted,

"Shit, it's the Bizzies. Stay there John!"

Before John could move, Alan sped off in a cloud of exhaust fumes, a blue and white police Ford Anglia in hot pursuit with blue light flashing and siren blaring. Round and round the block Alan went at ever increasing speed but with the police car gaining on the fugitives with each lap.

Each time they passed, the crowd of onlookers grew bigger. We were clapping and cheering and encouraging Alan and John to shake off their pursuers.

In desperation, each time Alan passed us we could hear him shouting to John,

"Jump off at the next corner. Just jump!"

John looked petrified mainly because of the speed Alan was doing even when turning the corners and was clinging on to the rear luggage rack like a limpet. But finally, Alan managed to gain some distance on the police car then slowed down sufficiently for the ashen faced John to attempt his dismount.

As he cornered for the umpteenth time into Aldford Road, John swung his telescopic , giraffe-like legs over the pillion as Alan slowed right down. Almost immediately, Alan accelerated at full throttle desperate to escape the advancing squad car and the attention of the increasingly exasperated pursuing police officers.

Unfortunately, what Alan didn't realize was that one of the turn-ups of John's massively flared trousers had become snared on the newly fitted luggage rack at the rear of the scooter. Oblivious to John's predicament, Alan continued to accelerate away from the scene of the crime with John hopping behind him on one leg. As Alan's speed increased, so did the length of John's hops as he was being towed along behind the scooter.

Needless to say the crowd of onlookers had grown considerably and was in uproar, laughing as John quickly had to increase the length of his hops to over thirty feet! Something had to give. Thankfully it was John's trouser leg which ripped off at the knee and carried on attached to the luggage rack. Meanwhile John dived into a nearby privet hedge for cover from the approaching police car, while Alan casually parked the scooter by the massed spectators after his final lap of the block.

The police car screeched to halt next to us and seconds later an incandescently angry young police officer approached Alan and shouted,

"Alright, who was Rudolph frigging Nureyev on the back of the scooter?"

As our Alan tried to look innocent, John appeared from his hiding place complete with his one trouser leg at half-mast. As the young constable was about to apprehend John and Alan, an older policeman emerged from the car and told his colleague to go back and radio in to the station to give their whereabouts.

We all stood with baited breath awaiting the senior officer's next move.

He circled the scooter studying and testing each part – tyres, brakes, lights and so forth. Finally, he stopped and looked intently at the Everton crests immaculately painted onto the side panels. The tension was unbearable as he turned and approached Alan and pointed at the scooter.

"Nice paint job – make sure it stays that way", he announced slowly. With that he winked at Alan, strolled over to the squad car and casually drove off amid cheers from the assembled crowd.

"Aren't our policemen wonderful?" we all thought.

OCTOBER 1970
STITCHED UP

The less than impressive start to the season for the first-team led to a fair amount of speculation in the media during September that Everton might be tempted to invest in one or two additions to their senior squad. Typically Sid McGuinness had his ear tuned to the grapevine and furtively let it be known that midfield utility man Tommy Jackson might be leaving as part of a deal to bring in a big name signing. Sure enough, not long after, the highly regarded and cultured midfielder Henry Newton arrived at Goodison Park from Nottingham Forest in exchange for £115,000 plus Tommy Jackson who moved the other way. Although Evertonians were sad to see the genial, popular Northern Irishman leave, it was generally accepted that Newton would provide additional guile and experience in the centre of the pitch. Jackson would, however, always be remembered for the reliable, dependable contribution he made as stand-in for each Everton's midfield Holy Trinity of Kendall, Ball and Harvey during the 1969-1970 Championship winning season.

Significantly and of more immediate concern though, was that the arrival of Henry Newton did not result in a continuation of Everton's improved form during September – quite the reverse. A disappointing 3-1 away defeat at Coventry City was followed by a lack-lustre 1-1 draw at home to Derby County. A 4-0 away drubbing at Arsenal was hardly the result Harry Catterick was looking for in the build up to Everton's European Cup second round, first-leg tie away at German Champions, Borussia Moenchengladbach the following Wednesday.

Against expectations, bearing in mind their recent form, Everton went to Germany and emerged with a well-deserved 1-1 draw and an away goal to take back for the return leg at Goodison Park at the beginning of November thanks to Howard Kendall. Encouraged by this favourable result in Europe, visitors Newcastle United were easily dispatched in a 3-1 win at Goodison with Howard Kendall on the score sheet again along with Joe Royle and Alan

Whittle. Sadly, this return to form was not maintained in the final league fixture of the month when West Bromwich Albion won comfortably by a 3-0 margin at The Hawthorns

This less than inspiring run of results during October left the Toffees in a position of mid-table mediocrity with very little to celebrate apart from a favourable result in the European Cup. It was clear though that Everton would struggle to overcome the powerful German side in the second leg without a huge improvement in form.

* * * *

After the 'B' Team match against Preston North End at the end of September, I had had a reaction in my previous ankle injury resulting in a painful swelling, which required further treatment over the following few weeks. Frustratingly, this meant I was declared unavailable for selection by physio Norman Borrowdale for the next two weeks. During this time I was encouraged by the fact that Ian Crawford popped into the treatment room every couple of days to keep tabs on my progress. He also kept me fully involved in 'B' Team match days even though I missed the games against Blackburn Rovers and Bury at the beginning of October. As a result I was back in training raring to go when the swelling had subsided and I was available for selection.

In a surprise move, Ian asked if I fancied playing in central midfield in the next fixture for the 'B' Team against Manchester United at United's training ground, The Cliff in Salford. He discussed the fact that George Telfer had been playing well as centre forward in my absence and said he had noticed that I was happy playing deeper in training matches and wasn't afraid to 'get stuck in' and win the ball in the middle of the park and had the speed to break forward and support in attack when required. I didn't need much persuasion as I told him I would play anywhere as long I got a blue shirt on a Saturday!

Although it was an unfamiliar position to me, I relished the more withdrawn role and the physical encounters in midfield. We held a strong United team to a goal-less draw and I returned along the East Lancs Road with some encouraging feedback from Ian.

In training the following week, Ian continued to play me in midfield in practice games and indicated that it might be a position I was more suited to. As it happened, I was given an unexpected opportunity to show Stewart Imlach and Tommy Casey what I was capable of not long after.

As part of the build-up and preparation for the start of the FA Youth Cup, Stewart and Tommy had arranged an impromptu practice match including a mixture of Reserve and 'A' Team players. Ian was asked to send a couple of his squad to make up the numbers in midfield and he had no hesitation in sending me and Mick Buckley over while he continued with his session at the other end of the training ground. I was happy to line up with Mick and Ronny Goodlass in midfield against seasoned professionals like Terry Darracott, Frank Darcy, Archie Styles, Harry Bennett and Gary Jones as well as new professionals like Peter Scott, John Smith and Billy Kenny.

Stewart took charge of our team and gave a few basic instructions about formation and positions and told me specifically to man-mark Billy Kenny. Tommy did likewise with his team and after that, blew the whistle for the match to begin. Now although this was a 'practice' match it was nonetheless highly competitive with players competing to be noticed by the Reserve and 'A' Team coaches as well the younger players pushing for selection for the FA Youth Cup squad. I was no exception.

It was a high speed, high octane affair with tackles and challenges flying in; and with a distinct lack of tactical input from either of the coaching staff. There was no stopping the game for the explanation of the technical or tactical subtleties to be illustrated for us. I was following my instructions to the letter – marking Billy Kenny very tightly and aggressively, to the point where he became increasingly frustrated about the close attention he was receiving from me. Other players got involved and tempers began the flare. As we tussled for one particular ball, the ball broke free and I flew into a tackle with John Smith. I managed to nick the ball away but the inevitable happened and John followed through and opened up a five inch gash right through to the shin bone of my left leg with his studs.

It was obvious from the reaction of the other players that I was hurt and needed attention, which I thought Tommy Casey was about to organise, when he blew the whistle to stop the game. But instead, he and Stewart Imlach lifted me to the side of the pitch where I was left while the remainder of the match was played.

I lay on the side of the pitch for about 15 minutes until the game was over before I was lifted by a couple of team-mates over to the treatment room and physio Norman Borrowdale was called to inspect the injury. He immediately rang Dr. Irving, the club doctor who arrived about 20 minutes later and stitched the gaping wound up. By this time my leg had swollen considerably and the doctor had great difficulty getting the edges of the gash close enough to stitch them together.

As the doctor was tidying up, the door from the corridor separating the treatment room from the trainers' dressing room opened and in walked Harry Catterick. After a brief discussion with the doctor, who explained the difficulty he had had in stitching my injury, he looked down at my shin and said, "That's a nasty knock that son. How many stitches have you had?"

I'm not sure, eight I think", I replied nervously.

The doctor nodded his confirmation of the number of stitches and added that I would be out for two to three weeks. Mr. Catterick left without saying anything else and went back into the Trainers' Room. As I got down slowly from the treatment table and was painfully trying my weight on my injured leg, I was aware of raised voices from the Trainers' Room. As Norman observed me pacing gingerly up and down, I could make out Mr. Catterick's angry voice saying, "That kid was left for 20 minutes. He should have had treatment straight away. He's had eight stitches. I don't care if it was a practice match, he might have broken his leg for all you know!"

It was obvious that he had been observing events from his office window vantage point above the training pitches. There were some mumbled platitudes from Stewart and Tommy but Mr. Catterick left leaving them both in no doubt about his feelings and slammed the door behind him.

****

In the three weeks it took for me to be back in full training, Stewart and Tommy didn't mention the incident. A case of 'least said soonest mended' for them I supposed. Meanwhile John Smith at least had the decency to apologise for what I hoped had been an accident. I did make a mental note, however, that if ever I was in that position again, I would make sure it wasn't me sporting stitches afterwards.

NOVEMBER 1970
PENALTY CLAUSE

The opening game of November was a key one for Everton. As well as it being a prestigious second round, second-leg European Cup tie against German Champions, Borussia Moenchenbladbach, the European Cup and the FA Cup represented the only realistic chances of the Toffees securing any silverware in a, so far, disappointing season. Indifferent league form had seen Harry Catterick's men win only five of their first fifteen league matches leaving them in an unaccustomed lowly position of 13th in the table and well adrift of pace-setters Arsenal and Leeds United.

So in many people's eyes progressing against the German Champions and having a good run in the FA Cup were essential if Everton's season wasn't to peter out as an anti-climax after their League Title the previous year.

The stage was set then for a Wednesday evening kick-off under the Goodison Park floodlights for Everton to face the powerful German side, which included outstanding players like Bertie Vogts, Gunter Netzer and their prolific forward Herbert Lauman in the squad. A tightly fought second-leg seemed guaranteed with the score poised at 1-1 after the first-leg in Germany.

After completing our pre match duties, the apprentices made their way up into the stands to enjoy the spectacle. Although well below capacity, Goodison was a seething mass of noise and chanting from both sets of supporters as Everton got the game under way.

Within 23 seconds, the Everton fans were sent into raptures when Johnny Morrissey cut inside from the left flank and sent in a teasing, swerving right foot cross aimed at the head of Joe Royle. The cross was too far in front of Royle for him to make contact but the curl on Morrissey's cross was sufficient to confuse Kleff in the Borussia goal with the ball going in at the far post.

Goodison Park reverberated as Everton, buoyed by the confidence their opening goal had given them, went in search of a second. Joe Royle was causing havoc in the German penalty area with his aerial threat, with Johnny

Morrissey able to go past his full back at will to provide a stream of accurate crosses from the left-wing. Kleff had to be at his best to deny Royle on several occasions and it only seemed a matter of time before Everton extended their lead.

Then, against the run of play, Moenchengladbach grabbed an equaliser to take into the half-time break after Andy Rankin, in an otherwise faultless performance in the Everton goal, failed to hold onto a cross delivered from a free kick and Lauman stabbed home from close range to give the Germans an unlikely equaliser on 34 minutes.

Tied at 2-2 on aggregate, the second-half was a succession of Everton attacks as they surged forward in wave after wave of attacks in search of a winner. The noise inside the stadium was deafening as Joe Royle, Johnny Morrissey, Alan Ball, Alan Whittle and Howard Kendall were all denied by the excellent Kleff in the Borussia goal. But it wasn't to be as, even after 30 minutes of extra time, the scores remained tied at the end of the match.

History was about to made as Everton and Borussia Moenchengladbach were to contest the first ever penalty shoot-out in a European Cup competition. This was a new experience for all concerned – players, officials, Managers; even the crowd seemed to seize the sense of occasion as the focus shifted to the Gwladys Street end of the ground and the volume inside Goodison increased to a crescendo as Joe Royle prepared to take the first penalty kick.

For once, Royle's trusty technique failed as he drilled his shot hard down the middle of the goal only to see Kleff beat the ball away to safety to the joy of the visiting supporters. Amid the raucous jeering of the Everton fans, Borussia's Seilhoff calmly slotted his spot kick past Andy Rankin to take the lead for the Germans before Alan Ball cooly levelled the score for Everton.

Pandemonium broke out next as Moenchenglabach's leading scorer Herbert Lauman put his penalty wide of Rankin's right-hand post. The scores were level at 1-1 after two penalties each. Hope was restored for the Goodison faithful. Johnny Morrissey was next up for Everton and the relief was palpable inside the stadium as he found the back of the net with his spot-kick. 2-1 to the Toffees and the pressure was back on the Germans but Heynckes was equal to it as he converted his penalty to square the scores again.

As the tension mounted once more, Howard Kendall drilled the ball to Kleff's right which brought the crowd to boiling point only for Koppel to make it 3-3 with one kick each left.

Some people couldn't bear to watch, as Sandy Brown stepped up to take Everton's fifth penalty. Everyone in the stadium held their collective breath as he took his run up and lashed the ball at unstoppable speed past the startled German 'keeper to restore the lead.

So it came down to German defender Muller to take the penalty shoot-out into 'sudden death' if he could convert his side's last kick. He placed the ball on the penalty spot as Andy Rankin set himself in the muddy goal-mouth and chants of 'Andy Rankin, Andy Rankin' echoed around Goodison Park. Muller hit his shot hard and true to Rankin's right. There seemed to be a moment's silence amid the bedlam as Rankin threw himself across the goal and beat the ball away to secure victory for Everton.

Goodison Park erupted.

As the celebrations rang around the ground, Andy Rankin was enveloped by team-mates and supporters alike as he was escorted triumphantly from the pitch towards a place in Everton folklore on a unique and historic night for the club.

The chaotic jubilation continued in the Home dressing room when the apprentices got down there to complete our post-match duties. The scenes were reminiscent of the ones seen towards the end of the previous season when the league title was within reach.

But no one was getting carried away – least of all Harry Catterick who was quoted after the match, in typical understatement, as saying, "I still say these penalties to decide a match are like a circus, but I can't think of a better answer apart from a third game".

Sadly the euphoria from that tumultuous night only lasted until Everton's next league game in which they took both points in a 1-0 victory at home against Nottingham Forest thanks to an Alan Whittle goal. An exciting but ultimately disappointing 3-2 defeat at Anfield in the Merseyside Derby was sandwiched between draws away to Stoke City and at home to Tottenham Hotspur which left Everton stranded in the lower half of the league table.

So a month that started with such a memorable and historic European victory for Everton ended with the defence of their League Title effectively over.

****

Thankfully, the gash in my shin had healed quickly and I was back to full fitness having only missed two 'B' Team games against Oldham Athletic and Tranmere Rovers. Equally pleasing was the fact that Ian Crawford selected me for the first game back after my shin injury at home to Preston North End, retaining my midfield spot, with George Telfer continuing at centre forward.

I was really enjoying playing in a deeper position with licence to get forward and did this to good effect against Preston scoring the opening goal in a free flowing 2-2 draw. Ian was very positive about my contribution in his debrief after the game reinforcing many of the points we had worked on in training.

I continued to work hard on putting Ian's advice into practice in the following days and weeks and found the change of position both enjoyable and a stimulating challenge. The additional motivation I had in working with Ian and playing in a new position meant I felt I had made more progress than at any time since I had joined Everton and was treating it as a last opportunity to prove myself during my last season as an apprentice. I also felt more tuned in to Ian's style of coaching. He certainly used a more cerebral approach than I was used to, taking time to explain the tactics he was employing and that gave me the confidence to try the new concepts and moves he was introducing his players to.

I took this renewed confidence into my next 'B' Team match at Bellefield against Bury, scoring all three goals in a 3-0 win, much to Ian's satisfaction.

"If you carry on like this, I'll have to recommend you for the 'A' Team", he said after the Bury match.

"You do that Ian. I won't let anyone down", I replied, meaning every word I said.

****

I sat two more 'O' Level papers at Childwall Hall County College in November. I hoped the results were going to be as positive as my foray into midfield for Everton.

DECEMBER 1970 COLD TURKEY

The inconsistency that had plagued Everton's season continued throughout another frustrating run of four league matches during December.

A tame 1-1 draw away at struggling Huddersfield Town thanks to an Alan Ball goal was followed by the only bright spot of the month when Southampton were overrun 4-1 at Goodison, Joe Royle scoring twice with Johnny Morrissey and Alan Whittle adding the other goals. Title challengers Leeds United were next up at home and Don Revie's team took no prisoners in a tetchy encounter with Leeds securing both points after holding on to a one goal advantage scored by Jack Charlton.

A disappointing 2-0 away defeat to a Derek Dougan inspired Wolverhampton Wanderers sent Everton into 14th position in Division 1 and completed a dismal first half of the league campaign.

It was difficult to put a finger on the cause of the decline in form compared to the previous season when the Toffees dominated the Championship throughout. On the face of it, very little had changed. Harry Catterick and Wilf Dixon were still at the helm and the tried and tested training and coaching philosophy and regime were being refined and repeated. The young Everton squad to all intents and purposes remained unchanged, in fact it was now more experienced having won the title with the added bonus of England international players having benefited from their World Cup tournament experience with England.

But changes had occurred. Andy Rankin had secured a long run in goal in place of Gordon West since the Keflavic European Cup tie at the end of September and Roger Kenyon had become a regular alongside John Hurst in the heart of the Everton defence replacing captain Brian Labone who had relinquished the captaincy to Alan Ball.

Whilst criticism could not be aimed at individual players – Rankin and Kenyon were outstanding at times and more than able replacements for their more experienced team-mates, it was perhaps more subtle factors that were at work. The calm assuredness of Brian Labone in defence was not yet evident in the emerging talent of Roger Kenyon. This was reflected in the number of goals conceded in the first half of the season with 39 goals against in 28 matches compared with 26 goals against in 30 matches in the 69/70 season.

Alan Ball's style of captaincy was different from Brain Labone's. His fiery temperament sometimes boiled over when his team-mates didn't meet his expectations or perform to his own high standards. We witnessed this at first-hand at Bellefield on a number of occasions during first-team training sessions when there were a few frank exchanges of view between Ball and some of his colleagues, which sometimes escalated into disagreements with Wilf Dixon, the first-team coach and notably once with Harry Catterick himself. Not a wise move on Alan Ball's part we all agreed. In some people's opinion, the captaincy also had a detrimental effect on Alan Ball's form with the added responsibility he was carrying detracting from his overall performances and influence on games in the first half of the season. An example of this was his goals tally. Up to the end of December, apart from his hat-trick against the part-timers of Keflavic, he scored only one league goal (against Huddersfield) compared with a total of eight over the same period of time during the previous season.

One point of concern was Mr. Catterick's health, which it was rumoured wasn't great. Nothing was ever discussed openly, and certainly not within earshot of the apprentices, but his appearances on the training pitches became less frequent and it was noticeable how much more of the work with the first-team was done by Wilf Dixon, sometimes assisted by Reserve Team coach Tommy Casey. The boss's gleaming white, stately Rover 3500 was increasingly missing from his 'reserved' parking spot at Bellefield, whereas it had been a virtual fixture at the training ground throughout the previous season.

Another factor was the issue of Everton's policy relating to transfers since their Championship winning season. Although Henry Newton had been drafted in from Nottingham Forest, there was little appetite from the board to bring in any other big name or big money signings for Catterick to blend into the squad. In fact, it seemed that the purse strings had been tightened considerably since the days when the club broke the English transfer record when Alan Ball was signed from Blackpool and Howard Kendall was plucked from under the nose of Bill Shankly. Instead, the Board were happy for more talent from within the ranks to be blooded. Apart from Roger Kenyon, a number of youngsters were introduced to the first-team squad for senior experience during the season including David Johnson, Terry Darracott and Mick Lyons.

However, one signing that went under the radar of most people was that of a young Welsh goalkeeper by the name of Dai Davies who was signed for £20,000 from Swansea City as replacement for Geoff Barnett who had previously departed for Arsenal . This largely unheralded signing was of little significance in the scheme of things at Everton at the time, but for me personally, it was to be of real significance a few months later.

Looking back at the end of December, no single major factor could be identified as the root cause of the malaise that had beset Everton's season and seen them fall so rapidly from the pinnacle of English football to relative obscurity in the lower reaches of Division 1. It was more likely to be a combination of forces and issues that culminated in their current situation. Only time would tell if this season was to prove to be only a temporary blip for Harry Catterick and his team.

On the positive side the draw for the Quarter Final of the European Cup saw Everton's spectacular penalty shoot-out win over Borussia Moenchengladbach rewarded with a mouth-watering tie against Greek Champions Panathinaikos in March. Plus, before that, January always brought the magic of the FA Cup.

****

I was determined to carry my improved form and confidence through into December with three matches against Blackpool, Liverpool and Manchester United to look forward to. After my hat-trick against Bury, I retained my place in midfield for the 'B' Team to travel to a cold and windswept Blackpool. In difficult conditions, George Telfer trumped my hat-trick in the previous match with one of his own and I kept up my scoring run with another goal to seal a convincing 4-1 win.

The following week I was buzzing in training. I couldn't wait to get out on the training pitch. The confidence that scoring five goals in my last three games had given me meant my motivation was sky high. I felt fit, strong and, above all, on a par with any of the apprentices at the club. I was ready to run through a brick wall if Ian Crawford had asked me to.

Next up was another mini-Derby match against the Liverpool 'B' Team at Bellefield in another keenly fought contest. We triumphed 4-0 and I can honestly say it was probably my best performance to date in a blue shirt. I covered every blade of grass on the pitch and tackled as if my life depended on it and also had a hand in two of the goals, which sent a well beaten Liverpool side home empty handed. Albeit a junior match, I didn't think there was a better feeling in the world than to be an Evertonian playing in an Everton team that had just beaten Liverpool.

Manchester United were our next opponents at Bellefield. United always presented stiff opposition and Ian asked me to play deeper and take up a position just in front of our back four that included a couple of trialists. The tactic worked perfectly and we won a tight contest with the only goal of the game.

That was five straight wins for Ian's 'B' Team at the end of a ten match unbeaten run and he wasn't slow in pointing out to Stewart Imlach how well his team was playing. After one training session, he called me over and said, "Stan I've been really pleased with you for the last few weeks. You've applied yourself well to a midfield role and you've even weighed in with a few goals. There's no game for the 'B' Team on Boxing Day so I've recommended you and George Telfer to Stewart to be in the 'A' team squad for their game against Oldham Athletic".

I was elated. The thought of playing alongside Ronny Goodlass, Mick Buckley, Ian Bacon and Ray Pritchard again, who were apprentices already in Stewart's 'A' Team Squad made me feel as though I was finally level with them after all the bad luck with injuries I had suffered the previous season. I couldn't wait for Saturday to come.

****

Monday mornings in the Apprentice's Dressing Room was always a great place to be – especially if we had been involved in a winning performance for the 'B' Team or the 'A' Team on Saturday. We would dissect the game, relive the highs and discuss our performances reflecting on what we might have done better or take the mickey out of anyone who had made an embarrassing mistake.

It was also a great place to be for listening to what we had all been up to socially or, in some cases, romantically over the weekend. On this particular Monday, just before Christmas, we were joined by Alan Wilson, one of our former apprentice colleagues, who had been promoted to the professional ranks of the club the previous season.

Alan held us spellbound as he recounted his story of how, on the previous Saturday evening, he had 'copped off' in the Grafton Rooms, a well-known nightclub in Liverpool, with a young lady with whom, shall we say, he became extremely intimate. Much to the delight of the testosterone-fuelled gathering of 15, 16 and 17-year-olds, Alan gave us a graphic description of the sexual shenanigans which ensued after he was invited back to her place, illustrated hilariously by various thrusts of his pelvis and imitations of her mutterings and moanings. Our misty-eyed drooling was only interrupted by the call from Stewart Imlach for us to get the balls pumped up for the morning training session.

"To be continued!" Alan said enticingly as he slipped out of our dressing room.

****

As we were fast approaching the Festive Season, it was no surprise when we were summoned up to the Players' Lounge at Bellefield for the annual meeting of all the playing staff with the hierarchy of the club to an address from Cecil Moores. In contrast to the up-beat assessment of the season to date prior to the Christmas of 1969 when Everton were riding high in Division 1, Mr. Moores was far more sanguine regarding what he described as 'the mixed fortunes' of the current campaign. Nevertheless he commended the Manager and all the players for their continuing efforts to bring further success to the club and reiterated the commitment of the Board to support the manager in the future, as and when required.

Also in contrast to last Christmas, he announced that, rather than a Luxury Christmas Hamper (including avocado pear), a large deluxe oven-ready Christmas turkey would be delivered the following day for each member of the playing and ground staff as gesture of goodwill from Everton Football Club to their employees. Needless to say that the following morning when the turkeys arrived, the apprentices were there like a shot, sorting out the biggest and plumpest birds before stashing them away in the dressing room prior to the pros turning up and collecting theirs.

As soon as the afternoon training session had finished, all the apprentices jumped into the showers and, while we were wrapped in towels and drying our hair, etc. Someone happened to remind us of Alan's hilarious anecdote about his new found love from his Saturday night out at The Grafton.

I don't know what got into me but, egged on by my fellow apprentices, I decided to re-enact Alan's escapades with his new girlfriend, using my turkey to assist. To roars of approval from the others and stark bollock naked, I cavorted around the dressing room with the oven-ready bird clamped to my knob, repeating the pelvic thrusts and mutterings and moanings that Alan had described.

Just as I was portraying Alan's climactic conclusion of his assignation and shouting, "Alan, more, more!", I was aware that the shouting and applause had suddenly stopped and I stood naked and alone in the middle of the apprentice's dressing room with my penis embedded up to the parson's nose in the Christmas gift from Everton Football Club to me and my family. I couldn't understand why it had gone so quiet until I turned to see Stewart Imlach standing with his hands on his hips, looking at me with an expression of bewilderment laced with disdain. After a tense few seconds, he shook his head, turned and left the room without comment.

After a moment's silence the dressing room exploded with laughter and piss-taking as I turned bright red with the embarrassment of it all.

The following day, the team-sheet for Stewart's Boxing Day 'A' Team fixture was pinned up on the noticeboard outside the dressing rooms followed by the usual stampede to see who had been selected. George Telfer was delighted to see his name included in the forward-line on the recommendation of Ian Crawford. My name, however, was nowhere to be seen.

Puzzled, I approached the Trainers' Dressing Room door and knocked before entering to find Stewart and the other coaching staff in a meeting.

I said, "Stewart, sorry to disturb you but why aren't I playing against Oldham on Boxing Day?" Quick as a flash, he replied, "I don't have turkey shaggers in my teams!"

JANUARY 1971
SWEET FA

There was no doubt that Evertonians loved the romance and magic of the FA Cup. Fresh in the memory of all but their youngest supporters was the epic 1966 triumph at Wembley against Sheffield Wednesday and the desperate disappointment of their defeat at the hands of West Bromwich Albion in the final two years later.

It was also an opportunity to shake off the disappointing league form that had beset the Toffees and set sights on a trophy they were still amongst the favourites to win. A Blackburn Rovers side who were struggling near the foot of Division 2 seemed the ideal opponents in the 3rd Round. And so it turned out with the Lancashire side being beaten comfortably at Goodison Park by a 2-0 margin with Jimmy Husband scoring both goals. This set up another favourable home-tie for Everton in the 4th Round later in the month against Middlesborough, also from Division 2.

Sandwiched in-between the two FA Cup ties were league matches resulting in a 2-2 away draw at Burnley, including a goal from up-and-coming young striker David Johnson and a convincing 3-0 victory at Goodison against a highly placed Chelsea side.

This improved form and results set up a confident Everton for their FA Cup clash against their visitors from the North East. An expectant crowd of 54,000, their biggest gate of the season so far, packed into Goodison Park for the tie and Harry Catterick's team did not disappoint as they ran Middlesborough ragged emerging with a resounding 3-0 victory. Yet another home draw for the 5th Round to be played in February saw Everton pitched against a useful Derby County side from the top half of Division 1.

Everton's unbeaten run since December came to an end in their last game of the month when they were narrowly defeated 2-1 at White Hart Lane by Tottenham Hotspur who were up amongst the leaders in the division.

The FA Cup had certainly added impetus to the season for Everton and their form was undeniably better in the matches following their win against Blackburn Rovers in the 3rd Round. The atmosphere in and around Bellefield improved as well. The players had a spring in their step and a smile on their faces; even the disagreeable spats on the training pitch seemed to diminish reflecting a budding optimism that something might be salvaged from the season – maybe some silverware..... just maybe.

* * * *

If the New Year heralded a period of optimism for the first-team, the opposite was true for my own hopes. Having had such a positive run of form during November and December, I was dismayed and disappointed to find that I was left out of the 'B' Team line-ups for matches against Bolton Wanderers and Blackburn Rovers at the beginning of January.

I felt that I was still training as hard as ever and doing everything asked of me in practice matches. After training one day I approached Ian Crawford to ask if there was any particular reason why I hadn't been selected. He explained that he was under instructions from Stewart Imlach to give a few games to a number of trialists who the club were interested in and that I had done nothing wrong. This didn't seem to ring true to me. To my mind it was ludicrous that I should be overlooked as a full-time apprentice professional in favour of amateurs who hadn't signed for the club. But who was I to argue? I just made my mind up to prove my point once I was selected to play again.

It did cross my mind though that my escapade with the turkey might have influenced Stewart's and, as a consequence, Ian's thinking.

The situation was compounded when Ian told me I was selected for the 'B' Team's next fixture against Tranmere Rovers but was told to abandon my new midfield role and revert back to centre forward as he was short of forwards due to George Telfer being retained in the 'A' Team squad by Stewart Imlach. By all accounts George had played really well since his promotion into Stewart's squad and thoroughly deserved his chance. I couldn't help feeling angry and dejected though because I hadn't been given the opportunity to play for the 'A' Team and show Stewart what I was capable of due to a bit of fun and high jinks in the apprentice's dressing room just before Christmas.

To make matters worse we lost our game at Tranmere 1-0 in a very disappointing game and I was dropped again for the following match against Oldham Athletic. The only bright point in an otherwise depressing month was that I led the 'B' Team forward line in another notable 1-0 victory against Liverpool at Bellefield.

But the joy of another win over our fiercest rivals was tempered for me by the realisation that I was out of favour, if not with Ian Crawford, then certainly with Stewart Imlach who held the key to any aspirations I had to play in the 'A' Team and thereby further my chances of becoming a full-time pro at Everton. I resolved to keep trying to impress Ian, whether in midfield or as a centre forward in the hope that Stewart might relent and give me a start in his team. After all, what else could I do?

My mood wasn't helped by the fact that, at about this time, Bobby Armstrong became the next apprentice to find out his fate as he was called for his interview with Harry Catterick to discuss his future. Bobby was a local lad from Maghull who showed tremendous potential as a schoolboy and played in the 'B' and 'A' Teams during his time at Everton. The expression on his face told the story when he returned to the dressing room to be consoled by the rest of the apprentices. Bobby was a good footballer and a really nice bloke – probably too nice, which was not something any of us could afford to be. A few days later Bobby had gone amidst stories that he might be joining non-league Southport.

I'd had another salutary lesson in the unforgiving, often brutal nature of professional football and its treatment of youngsters, where sentiment counts for little and nice guys seldom win.

****

On a brighter note, I was pleased when a brown envelope dropped through the letter box confirming that I had passed the two 'O' Level Exams I had taken in November. I'd have been far happier though if it had been a new contract from Everton.

****

My brother Alan had been working on the production line at Fords Halewood plant and was established on the Escort and Capri lines fitting the front seats. Working in a pair with his mate from Kirkby, Jimmy Farley, they enjoyed the usual workplace banter and Alan wasn't slow in describing some of the amusing incidents that often occurred.

One day he told me about how the foreman of his line had called a meeting of the workers that morning to tell them that some important visitors would be arriving from Germany at the plant that afternoon to observe the working practices in operation for the Escort and Capri. Alan and his co-workers were told it was all part of Ford's plan to rationalise methods of car production across their factories in both countries.

The foreman stressed that it was crucial that the workers were on their best behaviour and to be courteous to the VIP German visitors. Now bearing in mind the nature of industrial relations in those days and the fact that Germany was not the most popular nation in England following our dismissal from the 1970 World Cup, let alone the little matter of World War Two only 25 years before, the request for good manners and behaviour towards German big-wigs was something of a red rag to a bull.

Alan described how, when one of the German visitors arrived on the production line, he and Jimmy were working as they normally did, one at each side of a vehicle installing the front seats as it moved slowly along the line. The officious looking be-suited and bespectacled German stood observing the vehicle behind where Alan and Jimmy were working as a different component was added by two other workers, who carried on ignoring their observer as he studied his stopwatch and made notes on his clipboard papers.

He approached one of the workers and above the hubbub of the factory floor, Alan and Jimmy heard him ask in a loud, clipped German accent, "Haff you vorked on any off ze ozzer models in ze factory?" The worker indicated that he had, to which the visitor ticked a box on his paper and, without even a 'thank you', turned his attention to Alan and Jimmy.

So much for courtesy and manners they both thought.

They carried on their work as the German official watched intently for a few moments before he approached Jimmy, tapped him on the shoulder and asked, "Do you know who I am?"

Quick as a flash and without even looking up from his work Jimmy shouted, "Hey Alan! There's a bloke here who doesn't know who he is!"

FEBRUARY 1971 IFS AND BUTTS

The anticipation at the prospect of the FA Cup 5th Round tie to follow was palpable at Goodison as Everton overcame Huddersfield Town 2-1 in their next league match thanks to a brace of goals from an in-form Joe Royle. FA Cup fever had well and truly arrived the following Saturday as a crowd of over 53,000 at Goodison greeted an up-and-coming Derby County side managed by Brian Clough and his assistant Peter Taylor. In a very tight encounter, it proved to be memorable day for David Johnson who was replacing the injured Johnny Morrissey on the left flank. It was Johnson who scored the only goal of the game to send the Toffees and their delirious supporters through to the Sixth Round.

The up-beat atmosphere around Bellefield on Monday was buoyed further when Everton were handed yet another home draw, this time against fourth division Colchester United. There was no chance of any complacency on Harry Catterick's part though as he wasted no time in reminding his squad about Colchester's heroic encounter with Don Revie's mighty Leeds United at their Layer Road ground in the 5th Round. In one of the biggest upsets in FA Cup history, they had raced into a three goal lead only for Leeds to claw their way back into the tie with two goals, with Colchester hanging on to eliminate them in a classic David and Goliath giant killing act.

Returning to their league fixtures, a 2-2 draw with Southampton at The Dell was followed by a tightly contested Merseyside Derby where 56,000 saw honours shared in a goalless draw against Liverpool at Goodison Park. Two further home games in succession saw Everton take maximum points against Manchester United, thanks to a rare goal from full back Tommy Wright followed by an exciting 3-3 draw against West Bromwich Albion.

The points gained during the month meant that Everton's league position was stabilised at 10th with a buffer between them and the relegation battle that was developing at the foot of the table between the likes of Blackpool, Burnley, West Ham United and Ipswich Town. Full consideration could be applied at Bellefield to preparing for the potentially season-defining fixtures, which loomed in March.

If Everton could achieve a victory that seemed all but assured over Colchester, it would see Everton into another FA Cup semi-final. If Harry Catterick could inspire his team to a two legged win over Greek Champions Panathaikos, it would deliver a European Cup semi-final to Harry Catterick and his team. The Twin Towers of Wembley were almost in view again for Evertonians; European glory beckoned for the first time in their club's distinguished history; but only if the Gods were smiling on them. If only...

****

It was clear that time was running out for me at Everton. A quick look at the fixture lists told me that there were only a dozen or so matches for the 'A' and 'B' teams before the 1970/1971 season drew to a close in May. My eighteenth birthday and with it the end of my contract as an apprentice was in September. Along with the rest of the 1969 intake of youngsters, we hoped that we were on track to be recommended by Ian Crawford, Stewart Imlach and Tommy Casey for a full-time professional contract at the club. Realistically, my chances were slim. However much I thought I deserved at least a look-in with Stewart's team, I was still one of the few apprentices who hadn't made the all important breakthrough from the 'B' Team into the 'A' Team. Meanwhile, Ronny Goodlass and Mick Buckley were regulars and were even knocking on the door for inclusion in Tommy Casey's Central League squad. The likes of my Kirkby Boys team-mates Ray Pritchard and Paul MacEwan had made it into the 'A' Team as had Ian Bacon.

However, I wasn't daunted and refused to believe I didn't have a chance. I continued to train hard and have faith in my ability to become a pro.

I was handed the number nine shirt for the 'B' Team's next match away at Manchester City and was delighted to score the winning goal in a 3-2 victory but in yet another set-back I aggravated my old ankle injury again and was ruled out for the next two 'B' Team fixtures against Manchester United and Preston North End. Thankfully, I was able to keep up my scoring form when I returned to Ian's team for the final fixture of February, scoring the winner in a 2-1 win at home to Blackpool.

But although I'd scored seven goals in my last nine matches, something told me a call up to the 'A' Team was as far away as ever.

****

During my two week lay-off due to my ankle problem, I was being treated by physio Norman Borrowdale, when the photographers responsible for taking pictures for the first-team's match day programme arrived to take some photographs of Norman. He was to feature in the programme for the first-team's league game against Stoke City on 13th March in an article called 'Man At Work' which would focus on the important work done by Norman in getting injured players back to fitness.

After taking a few photographs of Norman in the physio room treating Gordon West for a thigh strain with some heat treatment equipment, the photographer asked if he could take some shots of Norman working outside. I was due to have a fitness test on my ankle that morning and was changed ready so Norman instructed me to join him and the photographer on one of the Bellefield pitches. After taking one or two pictures of Norman, he got me to do a test with me kicking the ball as hard as I could to test my ankle whilst he was blocking it with the sole of his shoe, as you would in a block tackle. After repeating this test and the photographer had finished clicking away, with no ill effects I was told to report to Ian Crawford and the rest of the apprentices to resume training. I didn't think any more of it – until the Monday after the Stoke City game in March.

****

Also during this lay-off, I was doing some strengthening work on my ankle with Norman, which involved doing astride jumps on and off an agility bench at the side of the indoor pitch. At the time, there was a practice match being played inside between a mixture of apprentices and young professionals – this was something that happened regularly during the winter months to save the pitches at Bellefield from excessive wear during the bad weather.

It wasn't unusual for these matches to get quite competitive and physical with many an unseemly aggressive confrontation between two young players resulting in a coming together and an ensuing exchange of blows only for the other players and coaches to intervene to quickly calm matters down.

I was no stranger to such confrontations myself having been disciplined during pre-season training after a clash with one of the other apprentices on Ainsdale beach. What was unusual about this match was that Stewart Imlach had decided to join in the match, which had been simmering gently as one or two meaty challenges and tackles had occurred. Surprisingly, Stewart had allowed himself to be embroiled in a tetchy exchange with young professional Alec Clark, who for some reason was playing outfield instead of in his goalkeeping position.

To everyone's shock after a heavy, clumsy challenge from Alec on Stewart, they squared up to each other and a fracas began. It was a pretty one-sided affair as Alec was six foot and Stewart only about 5' 7". The other players rushed to separate the pair but not before Alec had head-butted Stewart leaving him with gash on the bridge of his nose and the beginnings of two shiners developing.

Norman intervened and led Stewart away to his treatment room for attention to his injuries. I believe Alec's contract was not renewed when it expired – no ifs or butts!

MARCH 1971
BEWARE THE IDES OF MARCH

The 6th Round FA Cup draw really could not have been kinder to Everton – a home draw against giant killing minnows Colchester United, and so it proved. Harry Catterick had obviously done his homework and, with a swagger reminiscent of their best performances from the previous season, the Toffees turned on the style to overwhelm the fourth division side 5-0 with goals coming from Howard Kendall (2), Joe Royle, Jimmy Husband and Alan Ball. The immaculate passing and interplay throughout the team had the 53,000 Goodison Park crowd cheering to the rafters and starting to believe it was Everton's name that was on the cup. The only obstacle in the way of Everton returning to Wembley for the third time in six years was a semi-final at Old Trafford against arch rivals Liverpool at the end of March.

Three days after progressing in the FA Cup, the eagerly awaited first-leg of the European Cup quarter-final saw Greek Champions Panathinaikos visit Everton on an atmospheric evening under floodlights in front of a typically partisan Goodison crowd.

Everton started the game positively, pressing forward at every opportunity but were dealt a blow after seven minutes when Jimmy Husband was forced to withdraw through injury and was substituted by youngster David Johnson who slotted in on the right hand side of the attack. Everton continued to have the lion's share of the play but were unable achieve the breakthrough due to the stubborn resistance put up by the Greek Champions. As the game neared its closing stages, disaster struck when a long, hopeful high ball was launched into the Everton penalty area from a Panathinaikos defender, which Everton number five Roger Kenyon failed to deal with under the aerial challenge of the Greek centre forward. The ball fell invitingly for

157

Antonaidis who made no mistake planting the ball past Andy Rankin to give his team an unlikely 1-0 lead after 82 minutes.

The Goodison crowd were deflated as they faced the prospect of enduring a Greek tragedy with Panathinaikos taking an away goal advantage into the second-leg in Athens ten days later. Then, as the small contingent of Greek fans were calling for the referee to blow the final whistle, Everton were thrown a lifeline when substitute David Johnson skipped past his marker and ran on to score an equaliser in the Gwladys Street goal. The Goodison faithful roared their relieved approval. Johnson's goal had given them hope, but there was still a lot to do in the second-leg to secure a place in the European Cup semi-final.

After all the excitement of consecutive cup-ties, the three league fixtures before the return leg in Greece against Panathinaikos and the FA Cup semi-final versus Liverpool were something of an anti-climax.

In view of the fact that there was little resting on these games, Harry Catterick took the opportunity to rest some of his key players and give some experience to some of the up-and-coming youngsters in the Reserves. In their next match, a 2-0 win at home to Stoke, David Johnson retained his place for the injured Jimmy Husband; Johnny Morrissey was rested, with Alan Whittle coming in and Brian Labone was reinstated to the defence at the expense of Roger Kenyon.

A midweek trip to Newcastle saw Dai Davies, the new recruit from Swansea City given a start in goal in place of Andy Rankin and Howard Kendall rested with Sandy Brown replacing him in a 2-1 defeat. Catterick retained Dai Davies in goal for the following match at Nottingham Forest and rested Colin Harvey, giving starts to youngsters Billy Kenny and centre forward Mick Lyons, who got his name on the score sheet in a 3-2 defeat.

So the pivotal point in Everton's season had arrived. Within the space of four days, they could be in a European Cup Semi-Final and have marched on to Wembley and another FA Cup Final. Only Panathinaikos and Liverpool stood in the way.

In the build-up to the Panathinaikos match, flights and travel packages to Athens for fans had been advertised for weeks before. For example Shaws International Sports and Travel Limited (London), advertised their 'Soccer Special' packages in the Everton match day programmes including return flights from Speke Airport to Athens, transfers from airport to hotel and first class bed and breakfast accommodation, all for the princely sum of £32.50.

The excitement and optimism built as Harry Catterick set-off with his strongest side to do battle with Panathinaikos. But Everton's European adventure was to fail on a frustrating March night in the Greek Capital. Holding the away goal advantage from the first-leg at Goodison, the home side were content to contain and nullify all of Everton's efforts to secure the crucial away goal. Wave after wave of attacks were repelled by the obdurate defence of the Greek side and Everton returned home to Merseyside disappointed and crest-fallen.

Worse was to follow at Old Trafford three days later. Over 62,000 fans travelled along the East Lancs Road to Manchester to witness the FA Cup semi-final. In a worrying development, the Everton team were forced to make the trip without Manager Harry Catterick who, it was reported, was too ill to travel, instead handing responsibility to first-team coach Wilf Dixon.

In spite of their midweek exertions against Panathinaikos, Everton shook off their travel fatigue to start the match brightly and took the lead through Alan Ball on 11 minutes. Old Trafford rocked to the chants and songs of the Everton fans as they looked forward to putting their fiercest rivals in their place. But the game was turned on its head in the space of 14 second-half minutes when Alun Evans equalised for Liverpool on the hour and Brian Hall scored what proved to be the winner for the Reds.

Liverpool's fans danced and sang their way back to Merseyside to toast a famous victory, while Evertonians were left with the bitter taste of defeat for the second time in a few agonising days.

In the aftermath of the game, the fact that Harry Catterick was unable to be at the semi-final against Liverpool was a hot topic of conversation, as were Bill Shankly's comments at the time. Evertonians were rightly furious that Shankly was reported to have said that sickness would not have kept him away from the match... even if he was dead! Bill Shankly had many times over the years when the media and public were amused and entertained by what he had to say. This was not one of them.

But it wasn't Shankly's crass and insensitive remarks that hurt Evertonians the most. It was the realisation that the silverware that was so tantalisingly close had been snatched away at the eleventh hour and all that was left of the season was half a dozen or so league fixtures to fulfil. The mood was aptly illustrated when a dejected and tired Everton side capitulated at Goodison Park in their final match of March, to a struggling West Ham United side – the Londoners gratefully accepting two points courtesy of a Howard Kendall own goal. The only crumb of comfort for Evertonians came at the end of the season when Liverpool lost in the FA Cup to Arsenal in their famous double winning campaign and Panithanaikos were also beaten at Wembley in the European Cup Final by a Johan Cruyff inspired Ajax.

****

More in hope than expectation I continued to put in every effort with my training with Ian Crawford and the 'B' Team squad. I played in a 1-1 draw away at Tranmere Rovers and followed that up with a goal in a 1-1 draw at home to Burnley. Next up was a visit to Melwood for another mini-derby against Liverpool. Bearing in mind who the opposition were, I didn't need motivating for this fixture and was revved up at the start of the match. I had

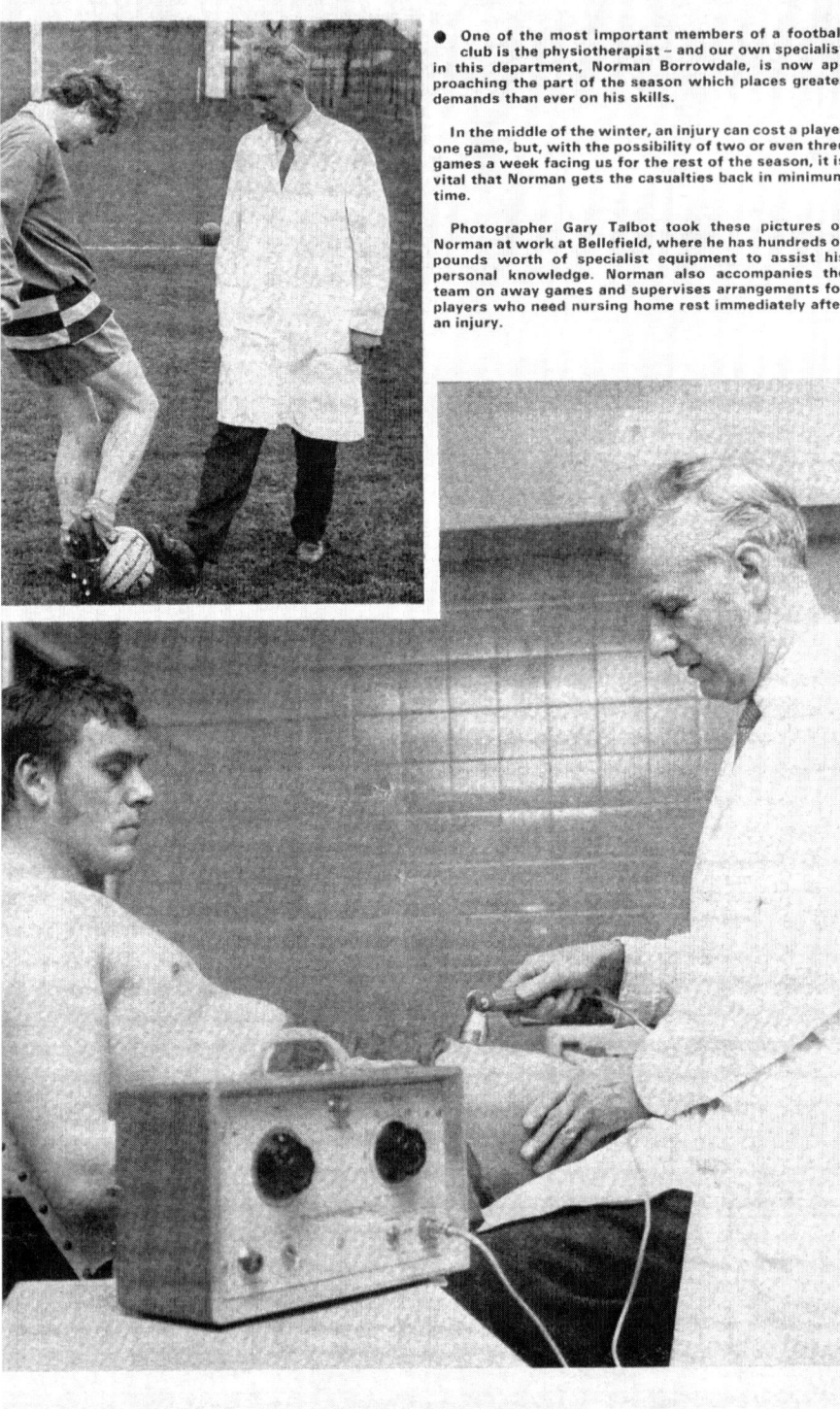

One of the most important members of a football club is the physiotherapist – and our own specialist in this department, Norman Borrowdale, is now approaching the part of the season which places greater demands than ever on his skills.

In the middle of the winter, an injury can cost a player one game, but, with the possibility of two or even three games a week facing us for the rest of the season, it is vital that Norman gets the casualties back in minimum time.

Photographer Gary Talbot took these pictures of Norman at work at Bellefield, where he has hundreds of pounds worth of specialist equipment to assist his personal knowledge. Norman also accompanies the team on away games and supervises arrangements for players who need nursing home rest immediately after an injury.

the beating of their centre half in the opening minutes and it wasn't long before I opened the scoring, latching onto a through ball and sliding the ball past the advancing goalkeeper.

Things became quite heated and I'm sorry to say, my temperament let me down again as I reached boiling point and I lashed out at the centre half resulting him having to be substituted and me being dismissed for violent conduct in a repeat of my last visit to Melwood. Reduced to ten men, a 3-1 defeat ensued, leaving Ian Crawford incensed at my lack of discipline.

Under normal circumstances a run of form which included a haul of nine goals in my last twelve games might have warranted a call up for the 'A' Team. Ian had said that he would have another word with Stewart Imlach prior to my sending off, but in view of my needless dismissal, I doubt that he ever did. Needless to say, the call from Stewart never came as George Telfer continued his excellent progress leading the line for the 'A' Team while I was left to ponder my future at the club.

****

In Everton's match day programme for the match at Goodison against Stoke City, the 'Man At Work' feature about Norman Borrowdale's duties as club physiotherapist duly appeared along with photographs of Norman treating Gordon West as he sat on the treatment table at Bellefield. Predictably, Norman got loads of stick from the pros about being famous and being very photogenic and the like, all of which Norman took in his usual dignified stride by telling them all to, "Bugger off and don't be so cheeky!"

Surprisingly, the feature also included a photograph of Norman with me, when we went outside to test the fitness of my ankle. Naturally, I came in for even more piss-taking than Norman, being called 'Big Time' for appearing in the programme. This escalated when I was in the young pro's dressing room next to ours. I was being mocked and jokingly asked to sign autographs, etc. But amongst the banter someone shouted, "I think that should be court case!"

There was a lull in the hubbub as they considered the suggestion. Quick as a flash, I grabbed one of the boots I was gathering-up ready for cleaning, turned and said, "F*****g try it and see what happens!" They didn't.

****

Although we apprentices had to take a vow of abstinence from alcoholic drink of any kind, it didn't stop us from enjoying ourselves when the opportunity arose. One Saturday I was invited to join my brother, Alan and his mate from Fords, Jimmy Farley for a drink (non-alcoholic for me) at the Sefton Arms in West Derby with the intention to go on to the Jolly Miller on Queens Drive and then back to Kirkby to a dance. We settled down with our drinks in the bar – Alan and Jimmy with their pints and me with my Coke.

After about ten minutes our conversation was interrupted by a voice from behind us that announced, "And I wonder what Mr. Catterick would think if he knew one of his apprentices was out on the town under-aged drinking!" I was frozen with fear but managed to turn slowly to be faced by the stern figures of none other than first-team players Joe Royle, Alan Ball and Howard Kendall, who were obviously out for a social evening following their match that afternoon. When they saw the terrified look on my face, they burst out laughing and pulled up some chairs to join us – to our astonishment! Here we were, three ordinary Kirkby lads out socialising with three Everton first-team players. It doesn't get much better than that... But better was to follow.

Howard Kendall had just got another round in and said, "Listen lads, we're off to the Wooky Hollow later. We've got some VIP party tickets – do you fancy joining us?"

Christ! Invited into a top club in town on a Saturday night as VIP guests with Royle, Ball and Kendall! Happy days we thought!

Quick as flash our Alan says, "Well we have had a better offer like – there's a disco on at one of the pubs in Kirkby, but if you're short-handed, we'll help you out like".

Cue gales of laughter.

Then disaster struck. A drunk (Evertonian) in the corner of the bar had obviously been observing events as they unfolded and recognised three of his heroes who were drinking with us. In a drunken stupor, he staggered towards our table slurring something like, "Awwwwlright Bally laaar. You're fuuuu**ing bossssss yoooooaaaaar!"

Then, in lurching forward to shake Alan Ball's hand he managed to knock our Alan's pint into his lap, soaking his trousers all down one leg. Not being of a very forgiving nature, our Alan had the drunk up against the wall by the throat in one movement.

"What the f**k do you think you're doing you soft get?!" he snarled.

He thought better of punching him and instead let him go as we watched him slide down the wall into an inebriated heap.

Not surprisingly, when we turned to speak to our three first-team companions, we were greeted with sight of the door of the bar swinging gently backwards and forwards on its hinges after they had made their exit – stage left. Crestfallen, dejected and disappointed, we made the best of what was left of the evening, but the pub in Kirkby and the girls we met at the disco there couldn't possibly make up for the chance of seeing how the other half lived as a VIP at a swanky Night Club. Sadly, we never did make it to the Wooky Hollow.

APRIL 1971
FADE OUT

Everton had difficulty in shaking off the sense of anti-climax that pervaded the club after being knocked out of the European Cup and FA Cup. In fact they were to win only one further match in their eight remaining fixtures. During April, a 3-0 home win against Coventry City, defeats away at Manchester City, at home against Wolverhampton Wanderers and at Derby County along with draws away at Ipswich Town and Blackpool left Everton only just above the relegation battle.

Harry Catterick continued to be an infrequent visitor to Bellefield, fuelling speculation that the health problems that had affected his attendance at some matches, including the semi-final against Liverpool, had not improved.

Considering Everton's form in the league had been poor all season, crowds at Goodison had held up reasonably well, but after their exit from both cup competitions, gates were well down with only 24,000 in attendance at the home win against Coventry City and 25,000 turning up for the final home match against Blackpool.

Meanwhile, the funding stream for transfers that accompanied the John Moores and Littlewoods association with the club had begun to dry up, leaving Evertonians to ponder what Harry Catterick would have to work with the following season. It was perhaps indicative that Catterick used the run-in to the end of the season to give more experience to promising Reserve team players. David Johnson had an extended run in the team and other players including Frank Darcy, Terry Darracott, Mick Lyons and Gary Jones were introduced to give them senior experience.

But in spite of the emergence of these promising youngsters, all was far from rosy in the Everton garden as the season limped towards its conclusion.

****

Likewise, my own season and with it my prospects of securing a contract as a pro were stumbling to an end. My final two games of the season for the 'B' Team resulted in defeat, firstly 3-0 at home to Blackburn Rovers and then 1-0 away to Burnley. It was an inauspicious end to a season in which I thought I had at least given myself half a chance of making the grade.

More apprentices were scheduled to be arriving soon and it was clear that the older apprentices would be told what their fate was to be in the not too distant future.

Davey Graham and former Kirkby Boys goalkeeper Keith Williams duly had their interviews with Mr. Catterick and returned empty handed, leaving the club a couple of weeks later with Keith saying he was going to explore the possibility of joining the Fire Service and Davey rumoured to be having a trial in non-league football.

That left me as the oldest of the remaining apprentices and logically that meant that I would be the next one to be invited up into his office to discuss my prospects. In spite of all the evidence to the contrary, I still refused to accept that all hope for me was lost and I continued to hold on to the faint possibility that I could be offered another contract.

MAY 1971
CLOSE THE DOOR ON YOUR WAY OUT

The final two games of the 1970/1971 season for Everton reflected the fortunes they had endured throughout the whole campaign. Their poor league form continued to the very end and concluded in a 2-0 away defeat at Crystal Palace, which meant that Everton ended up in a lowly 14th position. In their final fixture of the season Everton looked as tired and down beat as manager Harry Catterick when they returned to Selhurst Park a week later for the 3rd/4th place FA Cup play-off against the other losing semi-finalists Stoke City. In a match that only attracted 5,000 fans, Everton lost 3-2 with Alan Ball summing the whole occasion up by missing a penalty for Everton.

The contrast between this and the previous Championship winning season could not have been starker. A quick look at the statistics told its own story. Only 12 games won compared with 29 when they won the Championship, with 17 games lost compared with just five when they won the Title the previous season.

There was no escaping that this campaign represented a spectacular fall from grace for Harry Catterick and the Everton side he had successfully re-built and guided to their second League Title in six years. Tipped to be at the pinnacle of the English game for years to come, few would have predicted the outcome for the club at the end of the season. In spite of their sterling efforts in Europe and in the FA Cup, serious doubts emerged as the season unfolded about the ability of Catterick's team to mount a serious defence of their Championship crown and then go on to be the major force in English football that many Evertonians expected them to be. Their prospects seemed to be fading along with Harry Catterick's health.

Harry Catterick – "Right, you can go then. Close the door on the way out..."

* * * *

The start of the close season was a strange time at Bellefield. The weekly routine of training and preparation in the build-up to weekend fixtures was missing as the coaches wound down the intensity of the programme as players looked forward to their holidays. Having said that, there was no such thing as winding down for the apprentices. We were handed over to Dougie Rose and Sid McGuinness for large periods of time to begin the grounds maintenance work that was always required around the training ground during the summer months. Wheel-barrowing mountains of sand and soil around the pitches, painting goalposts and boot maintenance were the order of the day.

However, the training we did do with the 'A' and 'B' squads was light-hearted and enjoyable with skills and technique practice taking the place of exhausting shuttle-runs and five-a-side matches replacing timed cross-country circuits of the complex. All much more relaxed.

It was after one of the five-a-side matches, when we were showering and changing to go home, that Ian Crawford popped into the apprentice's dressing room and told me that the Boss wanted to see me in his office as soon as I was dressed. The look on everyone's face told me that they all realised what I had already assumed – it was my turn for the end of apprenticeship interview with Harry Catterick.

Even though I knew it was going to happen, the inevitability of being called for the interview didn't prevent a surge of adrenalin rushing through my body as I finished dressing and started my slow walk upstairs to Mr. Catterick's office. The narrow staircase to his office door echoed with each footstep as I made my way up them. I paused at the top, took a deep breath and knocked on the door. "Wait!" came the reply from within the office. I waited for what seemed an eternity, all the time wondering how I was going to react – whatever the outcome was to be.

Without warning the door opened and to my surprise it was Chief Scout, Harry Cook who beckoned me inside. The Manager's office was far smaller than I remembered it on the odd occasion I'd been sent there on an errand by the coaches or a fool's errand by the pros when I first started my apprenticeship. It was Spartan, with a Marley tiled floor, a couple of filing cabinets and two windows that met at right angles in the corner, each one with a clear view of Bellefield's two training pitches.

The room was dominated by a large desk, behind which Harry Catterick sat flicking through a pile of papers considering them intently. There was nowhere to sit so I stood across the desk from him waiting for the 'interview' to start, with Harry Cook standing behind him looking on impassively.

Mr. Catterick fixed his steely glare onto me and said calmly, "We're here to tell you whether you will be offered full professional terms at Everton". He tapped the pile of papers he had been looking through and added, "These are the match reports from all the games you've played since you've been at the club and we've discussed you with Stewart Imlach and Ian Crawford. We've made up our minds and we're not signing you and you'll be released at the end of your current contract. We can fix you up with a trial at Bolton Wanderers or Stockport County, but if I was you, I'd look for another job!"

I was devastated. Even at my most pessimistic, I never expected his assessment of my prospects to be so brutal. His last sentence cut right through me. As each word registered, it felt as if he'd torn out my Evertonian heart and squeezed every last drop of blue blood out of it until it was a dry husk and then thrown it to the floor to shatter, along with my dreams, into a thousand pieces.

"Have you got anything to say for yourself son?" Mr. Catterick asked, but I was speechless.

"Right, you can go then. Close the door on your way out...", he added coldly. As I turned to go, a single, huge tear ran down my cheek and splashed onto the floor. I was grateful that everyone had gone and the dressing rooms were deserted when I got back downstairs. I sat for half an hour or so trying to come to terms with the feelings of rejection and anger that were swirling round in my head as I went over what had been said to me. I felt worthless, a failure – a useless component in a huge machine, rejected and spat out onto the scrapheap.

As I walked along the driveway towards the gates of the training ground, the only other people there were head groundsman Dougie Rose and his assistant Sid McGuinness who were cleaning the grass off one of the large grass mowers they used to keep the pitches at Bellefield in pristine condition. Their expressions told me they already knew what my fate was. They always knew. If they always knew about big name transfers to the first-team, it stood to reason they would know which of the kids was signing or being released.

"Don't worry lad, there's better apprentices than you walked out of here when they were eighteen", Dougie observed, then added wryly, "And worse one's who've stayed". I shrugged my shoulders and wandered off in a daze towards the bus stop wondering how I was going to break the news to my mum and dad when I got home.

When I did eventually get back to Kirkby, my mum had just finishing cooking the tea so I waited until everyone had finished eating and waited for my dad to ask his usual question. "How did it go today?" He could tell from my expression that it wasn't going be my usual reply of 'OK' or 'Not bad'. He glanced momentarily at my mum, put down his paper and studied me closely.

"Harry Catterick told me I was being released Dad".

I'm not sure how I expected them to react. After I had described my interview with the manager and told them what had been said, my dad sat back in his chair, folded his arms and said, "Well all I can suggest is that you have a real good think about what you do next. Whatever you decide, we'll support you any way we can. But remember one thing. It doesn't matter what you do or where you go, there'll always be a home for you here".

My mum nodded her agreement and added, "I'm just glad you continued with your exams like Mr. Bury suggested. At least you've got something to fall back on".

The way I was feeling, it was probably the best thing they could have said to me.

****

It took a few days, but I soon came round to the idea that in only a matter of a couple of months, my apprentice's contract would be at an end and I would be leaving Everton after two years of living, eating and breathing football at the club I loved. As the pain and bitter disappointment had subsided slightly, I was able to think more calmly and rationally about what options were available to me when I did leave. I knew I had the bare minimum qualifications to go to Teacher Training College to train to be a

PE Teacher, which was what I had originally had thoughts of doing when I was at school, before the chance of joining Everton ever arose. On the other hand, the chance of a trial at another club was also a tempting idea, but I think subconsciously, I had already decided what I was going to do. After mulling it over in my own mind and discussing it with my mum and dad, they suggested I went back to Brookfield to have a talk with my old PE Teacher, Bob Downing.

Bob couldn't have been more helpful. We discussed trials, but I was still having problems with my ankle and wouldn't be happy going for a trial if I wasn't fully fit. Bob also explained that if I opted for an application for a place at college, time was against me as most colleges and universities finished their admissions procedures in June, leaving me very little time to apply. After speaking to Bob I weighed up the options before me and discussed them again with my mum and dad; a trial at another club with a dodgy ankle or applying for a place on a Physical Education Teacher Training Course. My mind was made up.

Within a week, I had made enquiries at Edge Hill College in Ormskirk and St Catherine's in Liverpool. They were both full but the administrators there suggested I send an application to the Clearing House System, which sent late applications to colleges nationally, which still had places on suitable courses to offer to students. Again Bob and Mr. Bury, my old Head Teacher were very helpful and were happy to act as referees in support of my application.

I felt a great sense of anticipation as my application was posted. Although the hurt and anger at my rejection from Everton were still fresh and raw, I felt a new opportunity and different journey lay before me and I was determined never to have to feel the pain of failure in anything else I did. Within weeks I would know the outcome of my application and whether or not I had been in time to secure an interview for the course I wanted, starting in the autumn.

JUNE 1971
HOWARD'S WAY

Most of the Everton first-team had already started their holidays. Just the apprentices remained to complete more grounds work before starting their summer break. Only pros nursing injuries were left to attend treatment sessions with Norman Borrowdale.

On a miserable, wet Sunday morning, I turned up as instructed at Bellefield to have treatment on my troublesome ankle. Having had to catch two buses from Kirkby in a virtual monsoon, the water was running down my back as I trudged up the driveway towards the entrance door. It was locked – Norman Borrowdale hadn't arrived and as there was nowhere to shelter, I huddled against the nearest wall cursing my luck and getting even wetter. Then, I was disturbed by the sound of what I thought was Norman's car approaching. But no, the large blue Jag gliding to a halt told me that it was in fact Howard Kendall reporting for treatment too.

Disappointed, I leant back against the wall looking forward to another drenching but, amazingly, the driver's window wound slowly down and Howard's head appeared. "Jump in", he said leaning over to open the front passenger door.

"Are you sure? I'm soaked", I protested mildly.

"Yeah go on, you're alright", Howard replied casually.

I jumped in quick as you like and sank into the soft, warm leather upholstery amazed that one the first-team players would allow a snotty, soggy apprentice near his top of the range Jaguar interior.

Howard said, "I hear you're on your way soon".

"Afraid so", I replied, half embarrassed that he knew that I had been the recent recipient of one of Harry Catterick's famous career development interviews. I explained how my interview had been short and not very sweet.

I went on to tell him how, although the outcome of the interview wasn't exactly a huge surprise to me, I was still gutted that my dream was coming to an end and my illusions had been shattered.

Howard listened patiently to my outpouring and then asked," What are you going to do?"

I told him that I had decided to use the exams I had managed to pass to apply for a place on a Teacher Training Course as a PE Teacher and that I was hoping to hear in the next few days whether I had been called for an interview.

Our conversation was interrupted by the arrival of physio Norman Borrowdale, who opened up and we dodged the pelting rain to go inside and wait for our treatment.

To my surprise, when I emerged into the car park afterwards, Howard was still there in his Jag – and the rain was even heavier. I started to make my way down towards the Bellefield gates when Howard wound down his window again and said," I'll drop you off at home if you like". I wasn't arguing and dived into his Jag again.

On the way back to Kirkby, Howard explained that new goalkeeper, Dai Davies had qualified as a teacher prior to joining Swansea City and then being signed by Everton. He said that he thought Dai might be able to help me with my preparation for my college interview if and when it was confirmed I had got one.

By this time we were approaching Aldford Road and the rain had stopped. As we pulled up outside our house, my mum was just emerging from the front door to nip over to Frank Ainsworth's van to do some shopping. She nearly fainted when she recognised Howard and saw me getting out of his Jag.

"Is that your mum?" Howard asked.

"Yes, why?" I answered.

He got out of his car and walked up to my mum and said, "Mrs. Osborne, I hope you don't mind, I've dropped Stan off to save him getting soaked again".

My mum was speechless but just about managed not to prostrate herself before him and thanked him for his trouble. It was surreal – Howard Kendall, an Everton legend, apologising to my mum for going about twenty miles out of his way to give me a lift back to Kirkby from Bellefield!

A couple of days later, my letter arrived from the Clearing House along with a letter from West Midlands College of Education in Walsall inviting me to an interview the following week for a place on their PE Teaching course. The timing couldn't have been better and I managed to catch Dai Davies who offered to arrange a 'mock interview' to put me through the sort of questions I was likely to encounter when I travelled to Walsall seeking a place at West Midlands College. Dai was a huge help, giving lots of feedback on the answers I had given and pointing out the key areas I needed to brush up on before I attended my interview.

The help he gave me paid off. I was elated when I was offered a place on the Teaching course for Physical Education and couldn't wait to get back to Bellefield the next day to tell Howard Kendall. When I found Howard, I thanked him for all his help and support and for putting me in contact with

Dai Davies. Typically, he just dismissed it as if it were nothing and wished me all the best with my new career. As all the apprentices knew, that was just Howard's Way.

****

I was surprised that it was Stewart Imlach who broke the news. I expected it to be Ian Crawford. He called me across as we were finishing some goalpost painting during the last week in June.

"Stan, we're going to let you go at the end of next week. There's no point in you being here, when you'll be going to college in a couple of months. I've had a chat to the Boss and he agrees that it makes sense for you to be preparing for that", he explained.

"What about my wages?" I enquired.

"That'll be taken care of. Your wages will be delivered recorded delivery to your home address every week so you'll not lose out. You might even be able to get a temporary job in the meantime to get some money together before you start at college", Stewart continued.

"We've got some new lads starting next month you see." he added.

There was an embarrassing pause before I said, "That's it then?"

"Afraid so son", he replied with a shrug and then added, "Good luck with everything", before heading off towards the changing rooms.

I wanted to call Stewart back and ask him what he'd said to Harry Catterick when they were discussing me. Realistically, I think it might well have been something like, 'He's quick, but a bit injury-prone; can score goals but his temperament is too fiery; too handy with his fists and not handy enough with his feet'. In all honesty, I couldn't have blamed Stewart if that was the case and although I tried, I couldn't really hold a grudge against him. He had a job to do and part of that job was to make judgements, however tough, about the youngsters at the club. That was the harsh reality and we were all under no illusion about that. This was Everton Football Club after all and that, literally, meant only the best was good enough. Clearly I wasn't.

Although I was angry, I didn't feel any animosity towards Stewart or Everton – I still loved the club in spite of everything – my anger was with myself. I riled at the thought of letting this once in a lifetime opportunity slip through my fingers and cursed myself for failing; for simply not being good enough to make the grade. I longed to turn the clock back to that July day in 1969 when I walked into Bellefield for the first time, but to be armed with the knowledge I had gained through bitter experience over the past two years. If that had been the case, I wouldn't have had any more natural ability as a footballer but there is no way I would not have made the grade because all of the pitfalls would have been known to me – a classic case of 'if I'd known then what I know now'.

I wanted to stay and tell the new apprentices who would be taking my place about what the pitfalls were that they were bound to face. I wanted to wish them luck in avoiding any serious injuries and tell them to avoid falling out with any of the coaching staff and develop a positive relationship with them, currying favour whenever possible. I wanted to warn them about the intimidation they were likely to experience and advise them to grow a thick skin, become self-centred and ruthless. I wanted to tell them to look after themselves first and assume nobody was going to do them any favours. I wanted to urge them to keep their discipline, be the fittest, strongest, fastest they could be and work harder than anybody else to improve their skills and technique. I wanted them to realise that football was a 'dog eat dog' business where only the fittest survive and the club has the luxury of discarding all but the best of the best. These were all things I knew at seventeen but wished I'd been told when I was two years younger.

JULY 1971
IF THE
LABEL FITS

Only the apprentices and the ground staff were left at Belle-field putting the finishing touches to the preparation of the training complex prior to pre-season training beginning for the start of the 1971/1972 season, before they too were sent away for their short summer holiday.

It was my last day so I spent the afternoon disposing of my training gear back into the 'recycling' box in the drying room. I gave my match boots one last clean and wrapped them in a plastic bag ready to take home. My training boots were on their last legs so they ended up in the bin.

I popped back into the apprentice's dressing room to say my good byes to the lads who wished me all the best. Lads who started their apprentice-ships at the same time as me; Liverpool lads, Ronny Goodlass and Ian Bacon, fellow Kirby lads Ray Pritchard and Paul McEwan, and Mancunian Mick Buck-ley who all knew that they would either soon be following me out of the exit door or be one of the chosen ones to continue their careers as a pro at Everton. I could see it in their eyes.

The last person I spoke to before I left Bellefield for the last time, appro-priately, was Jim Tansey, the Everton scout who first spotted me playing as a schoolboy in Kirkby. He made a point of speaking to youngsters who were being released before they left. Before shaking my hand, he wished me luck in the future and told me that he was sorry it hadn't worked out for me at Everton. He added that in his experience, being at a club like Everton was something that would have a bearing on the rest of your life; that the Everton label stuck wherever you went and whatever you did. It was a small crumb of comfort to take with me as I tucked my boots under my arm and headed for the gates.

I had walked in a naive, innocent, starry-eyed schoolboy with a hint of talent in his feet. I walked out a case-hardened, hard bitten, angry young man with chip on his shoulder the size of the Liver Buildings who was deter-mined never to feel the pain of failure again in whatever I did in the future.

My love of Everton had been strained during my time there but it remained undiminished. However briefly, I'd lived the dream; I'd rubbed shoulders with legends and had a fleeting chance to be one of them, but come up short – like thousands of kids before and since who had dreamed of making the grade.

* * * *

This book represents a very personal recollection of the most intense, challenging, inspiring and ultimately frustrating two years of my life. Even forty years on, the memories are vivid and vibrant. I hope I have portrayed a picture of what life could be like for an apprentice at a top club during that era and, even allowing for the passage of time, that it is an accurate reflection of a short episode in the history of a great football club. A history I am proud to say I was a very small, insignificant part of.

BACK TO THE FUTURE

I n the forty or so years that have intervened since I walked out of Belle-field for the last time after being released by Everton at the end of my apprenticeship, many things have changed at the club. Players, coaching staff, managers, even the ownership of the club have all been subject to the ebb and flow of change, which has seen the club delivered from a seemingly simpler and more innocent time into football's modern era.

After Harry Catterick, first Billy Bingham, then Gordon Lee, Howard Kendall, Colin Harvey, Mike Walker, Joe Royle, Walter Smith and now David Moyes have all occupied the managerial hot seat at Goodison Park – with varying degrees of success. Only the domestic and European glory years of the 1980's under Howard Kendall and the FA Cup Final victory secured by Joe Royle in 1995 saw silverware arrive back at Goodison while Everton's fortunes have risen and fallen as top flight football in England was transformed over time into the cash-soaked Premier League we have today.

The days of Everton being dubbed the 'Merseyside Millionaires' under the Chairmanship of John Moores are long gone, but in spite of no longer having the benefit of a wealthy benefactor, the club have maintained their top flight status and remain an iconic name in the English game. Nevertheless, new investment remains an urgent priority if Everton are to compete for trophies with the wealthier members of the Premiership once more. This situation is exemplified by Goodison Park. In the 1970's it was considered to be the pre-eminent ground in the country boasting a list of modern, cutting-edge facilities and features, which meant that Everton continued to be leaders of innovation in stadium development nationally. Now, although nicknamed 'The Grand Old Lady' and steeped in atmospheric and nostalgic tradition, she now falls well below most top flight grounds for facilities and is thought by some to be a major factor inhibiting the attraction of new investment into the club. Evertonians, myself included, hope that new investment is forthcoming and that Goodison Park, and with it our fortunes as a force in English football, can be developed securely into the future.

One thing that hasn't changed about Everton is the club's tradition of identifying and developing new talent, which has continued unabated. Each generation has seen a fresh crop of youngsters come through the ranks into the first-team. Players like Peter Scott, Mick Buckley, Ronny Goodlass and George Telfer from my era. Mick Lyons, Terry Darracott, Kevin Ratcliffe, Derek Mountfield, Michael Ball, Richard Dunne, Leon Osman, Tony Hibbert, Wayne Rooney, Jack Rodwell – the list goes on........

What then of Bellefield, the place where these players were nurtured? What of the place I had spent two years of my life trying to be one of them?

A trip down memory lane to that particular leafy corner of suburban Liverpool found me at the entrance to a modern estate of smart detached executive homes. The pristine pitches and gleaming goalposts of Bellefield have been replaced by neatly tended flower borders and trellis fencing. The hum of domestic lawnmowers hangs where the raucous shouts and banter from Everton training sessions once cut the air.

After 61 years associated with their West Derby training ground , Everton's last training session took place in 2007, the gates were closed and the land sold for development and a rich chapter in the history of the club came to an end as Bellefield surrendered to the bulldozers. The decision had been made to consolidate the club's training facilities by bringing together their Youth Academy facility and first-team operations at one site within a £14m development at Finch Farm near Speke.

* * * *

Finch Farm is a truly world-class facility. You cannot fail to be impressed as you enter the site via the sweeping tarmac driveway to be met by the gleaming glass, brick, concrete and blue tiled exterior of the main building. The sheer size of the complex hits you immediately – ten full size pitches (all of identical dimensions to Goodison Park), two mini-soccer pitches and an all-weather pitch, all laid out immaculately like photos from a glossy promotional brochure.

Inside the main building a long corridor is lined with action photographs of past graduates from Everton's Academy – Osman, Rooney, Rodwell et al, who have made their way via the Everton production line into the first-team – a reminder, if any were needed, of how successful the club has been at bringing players through the ranks. A plan of the complex outlines an incredible array of facilities – all aimed at providing Everton's youngsters with the best possible equipment and support in the development of their potential. Facilities including a gymnasium with every conceivable piece of specialist equipment to aid physical conditioning; a state-of-the-art medical and physiotherapy centre; five star dining facilities – the list seems endless.

On reflection, it occurred to me that Finch Farm made Bellefield seem quaintly old-fashioned; a relic from a different time and place – 21st Century technicolour with digitally enhanced 3D and surround-sound versus black and white or sepia mono-tone.

Whilst prospective players in my day were given our booklet 'Everton & You' to illustrate what an apprenticeship might have in store for us at Bellefield, a plethora of detailed information is available to talented youngsters and their parents on Everton's Club website outlining what they might expect as a member of today's Finch Farm Academy. The Academy Structure is laid out: Technical Development (Coaching), Identification and Recruitment (Scouting), Medical (Physiotherapy and Rehabilitation), Sport Science (Psychology, Physiology, Performance Analysis), Education and Welfare (Life Skills), and Administration and Facilities Management. Clearly no area of development has been left to chance and the structure and facilities at Everton's new complex reflect this. It is also interesting to note what Everton have described as the 'four corners of elite player development', namely:

- Technical: Skills development appropriate to a player's age and maturity.
- Physical: Fitness and athletic performance.
- Welfare Issues: Diet, nutrition, alcohol and drugs abuse, time management, gambling, bullying and handling the media.
- Mental: Goal setting, motivation, self-confidence, concentration, communication.

Such a wide reaching structure and detailed and well-resourced approach to player development obviously requires an incredible range of expertise for it to be delivered effectively. The staffing structure at Finch Farm mirrors this need with an array of scouting staff, medical practitioners, fitness trainers and performance analysts all represented as well as traditional coaching and management staff. An army of grounds maintenance and kit staff must also be needed to keep Finch Farm in top order. This seems such a huge and incredibly sophisticated operation and reflects the demands on a top Premier League club in the modern era. It also seems a far cry from the Everton of 1969/70 when Harry Catterick, Wilf Dixon, Arthur Proudler, Tommy Casey, Stewart Imalch, Norman Borrowdale, Dougie Rose and Sid McGuinness were the only people players would come into regular contact with at Bellefield on a day to day basis!

And what of the talented youngsters who are lucky enough to be spotted by Everton and to be taken on at the latest manifestation of The School of Science? What is their journey from talented schoolboy to first-team pro likely to hold for them these days?

Firstly, their journey will almost certainly start at a much earlier age with clubs identifying youngsters as young as six years old to be recruited. They are introduced to organised small sided matches at the age of nine and have their progress in all aspects of their development closely scrutinised and monitored. By the time a player reaches the age of 16 and is either signed as a full-time player or released he might have been with the club for ten years! Throughout that time youngsters have to perform to exacting standards in order to be retained and stay on track to achieve their ambition to be a professional footballer.

Ray Hall, Everton's Academy Director, describes how difficult it can be for players to break through in the modern game using the following analogy on the club's website: "To become a full-time player at Everton at the age of 16 or 17 is the equivalent of getting to Oxford or Cambridge. Getting into the first-team is like becoming Prime Minister."

There in a nutshell is the fundamental truth about how difficult it is and always has been to make the grade as a player. Somewhere along the line, in spite of all the lavish facilities and diligent care and attention given to young players, harsh, hard-nosed decisions have to be made. The unavoidable fact of footballing life is that you know hearts will be broken and dreams will be shattered for all but the chosen few. Been there, done that and gosh the tears hurt... even now. Some things it seems never change.

After seeing the set-up first hand at Finch Farm, it will be evident to anybody that Everton are determined to unearth more hidden football gems from within their ranks. As always, only the best will be good enough and competition will be as fierce as it has always has been for players lucky enough to be given the chance to prove themselves. I wish them all luck as they begin their journey and envy them their opportunity because from where I'm standing after all this time and for what it's worth, I would say that the future of The School of Science is still in safe hands.

SCHOOL OF SCIENCE, THE CLASS OF 68-72

WHAT HAPPENED NEXT ?

Peter Scott (Kirkby Boys): Played 48 games for Everton's first-team and gained 10 caps for Northern Ireland before going on to York City and then Aldershot. He was last heard of believed to be working in the pub trade.

Joe Moran (Liverpool Boys): Wasn't signed on as a pro. He was believed to be considering a job as a motor mechanic. He played in non-League football on Merseyside for a while. If loving Everton had been a criteria, Joe would have made the grade without doubt. Now sadly deceased.

Keith Williams (Kirkby Boys): Keith didn't make it as a goalkeeper at Everton. It was rumoured that he was pursuing a career in the Fire Service. No information regarding his playing career.

Alan Wilson (Liverpool Boys): Two first-team appearances before moving to Southport and then Torquay United.

David Graham (Sefton Boys): He was released at the end of his apprentice contract. No information about his career after he left.

John 'Tigsy' Smith (Liverpool Boys): Played twice for the first-team before moving to Carlisle United and Southport.

(Left to Right) Mick Buckley, Ray Pritchard, Peter Whitwood, Harry Catterick, Ronny Goodlass, Stan Osborne, Ian Bacon

Les Ormrod (Manchester Boys): Not signed as a pro at Everton but went on to play over 100 games for Stockport County before having spells at Northwich Victoria and Macclesfield Town.

Bobby Armstrong (Ormskirk Boys): Not signed as a pro at Everton and went on to play non-League football – clubs unknown.

Ronny Goodlass (Liverpool Boys): Made 47 first-team appearances before being transferred to NAC Breda and then Den Haag in Holland. Returned to England playing for Fulham in the 80/81 Season, then briefly at Scunthorpe United. He then had a spell playing in Hong Kong before finishing at Tranmere Rovers in the 84/85 Season. Ronny now commentates on Everton matches for Radio Merseyside.

Ray Pritchard (Kirkby Boys): Ray was released by Everton at the end of his apprenticeship and trained as a fitness instructor. He had a spell at Tranmere Rovers before playing extensively in non-League football on Merseyside for Marine, Southport, Runcorn, Bootle and Formby. Passed away in 2003.

Ian Bacon (Liverpool Boys): Ian secured a pro contract at Everton but didn't make it to the first-team. Emigrated to Australia and had a succesful spell playing down under before returning to the UK and settling back in Liverpool.

Paul McEwan (Kirkby Boys): Released at 18 by Everton then studied and qualified as a PE Teacher. Paul left Teaching to concentrate on his golf and eventually ended up as Senior PGA Club Professional at Birchwood Golf Club near Haydock.

Mick Buckley (Manchester Boys): Mick was the most successful of the batch, eventually playing over 300 matches as a professional. 149 were for the Toffees followed by 121 for Sunderland. Mick then went on to play for Hartlepool United, Carlisle United and ended his career with Middlesborough.

Peter Whitwood (Grays & Essex Boys): Left Everton after a year and returned to Essex after being unable to settle on Merseyside.

George Telfer (Huyton Boys): George played 91 games for Everton before trying his luck in the USA at San Diego. He returned to England and played for Scunthorpe United, Altringham (non-League) and had a brief spell at Preston North End.

Jimmy Burns (Kirkby Boys): Didn't make it to a pro contract at Everton. No information about his career after he left.

Stan Osborne (Kirkby Boys): Released from Everton at 18 and trained as a PE Teacher. After leaving college, he played semi-pro at Sutton Coldfield Town in the West Midlands. He finished his teaching career as Head Teacher at a Primary School in Smethwick.